Palaces, Patronage & Pills

Thomas Holloway: His Sanatorium, College & Picture Gallery

John Elliott

First published in 1996 by Royal Holloway, University of London, Egham, Surrey. Redesigned and reprinted in 2006.
Design and typesetting by The Design Studio, Royal Holloway, University of London.
Printed by APG, Unit 9, Mitcham Industrial Estate, Streatham Road, Mitcham, Surrey CR4 2AP.

Front cover image: The Great Hall after restoration, former Holloway Sanatorium. Opposite: Original wallpaper from the Boardrooms, Royal Holloway, University of London.

British Library Cataloguing in Publication Data. A catalogue record for this book is available from the British Library.

ISBN 0 900145 99 4

Acknowledgements

As you drive down the A30 towards Egham you will see Holloway's College on your right. You may not know that this is part of the University of London but you certainly cannot miss the French château style buildings which dominate the skyline. Similarly as you drive up the M3 from London after dark you can see the tower of Holloway's Sanatorium lit up and highlighted against the sky, and it certainly looks spectacular. When you see the inside of these two remarkable buildings and visit the Picture Gallery at the College or the Great Hall at the Sanatorium you are in for an even greater surprise. Both are historically important and both breathtaking in their own way.

These two buildings stand as icons of the Victorian age, of its enterprise and confidence and of a truly remarkable man who was determined to leave his mark as a reminder to later generations. They also stand as examples of Victorian philanthropy, and of a desire to give something back to the wider community, a concept that seems strangely out of place in our current age.

The College is part of the University of London and has been since 1900. The Sanatorium is now known as Virginia Park. It passed from being a private hospital to part of the Health Service and continued as a mental hospital until 1981 when new drugs and changing attitudes made 'Care in the Community' the norm. A series of failed development attempts followed and the buildings degenerated till Octagon Developments acquired the site in 1994. In exchange for restoring the main structure Octagon were given permission to develop the site for residential use. The purists may have considered it all a compromise but it was an agreement that guaranteed this remarkable building an assured future.

My intention here is not to provide a comprehensive history of the College or the Sanatorium; the latter still awaits an author, while the former was produced in 1987 by Caroline Bingham. Neither is this book intended to supply a catalogue for the picture collection, that having been produced by Jeannie Chapel in 1982 and reprinted in 1994. Finally, it was not my intention to document the Holloway family history, since that has already been done by Anthony Harrison-Barbet, a distant relation of the Holloways.

Instead this book arose from lectures and talks I have undertaken on Holloway, his College and picture collection; talks which usually led to at least some of the audience asking which single book they could buy to gain an overview of this remarkable Victorian philanthropist. They did not want the lengthy and exhaustive history of the College, they did not want a detailed family history, they did not want to know about every picture in the collection, but they did want to gain a perspective of the man, his business affairs and his charitable activities. In short they wanted a brief but comprehensive account of how Holloway made his money and how he spent it; how and why the Sanatorium and College came to exist, and how and why Holloway created a picture collection.

These are the reasons for this book, and these the answers it is intended to provide. It is not an academic textbook but neither is it intended simply to grace the coffee table; instead it attempts to chart a middle road, serious but entertaining, compendious without being voluminous. It also attempts to merge pictures and text, as any other method seemed inappropriate for a subject dominated by questions of art and architecture, subjects that are essentially visual. Perhaps most of all the book is intended to be an enjoyable read, one that will help to enhance the reputation of this remarkable Victorian and his little known architect, while also enlarging public knowledge of two very remarkable buildings.

This book was first published in 1996. Amazingly it has sold well. This revised edition of 2006 contains some amendments to bring the text in line with recent happenings plus some new photographs. The design has also been changed to ensure that the original and new editions are visually distinctive.

In producing the book I have incurred many debts of gratitude. Professor J Mordaunt Crook, Dr Mary Cowling and Janet Gunn all guided me through the writing process, while Sarah Roddy, Cyp da Costa and Sarah Hilliar did the same during the design process. Sophie Banham and Helen Haynes were enormously helpful in giving me access to original Holloway and College archive material. Graham Dennis and Richard Williams helped me to develop my ideas and to contrast them with their own.

Special thanks also go to Jane Faust, PR Consultant to Octagon for providing photographs of the Sanatorium.

However, it was Marta Baker who always believed in the marketability of the book and the fact that we are now producing a reprint vindicates her vision. Throughout ten years she has been a constant support and has done more than anyone to disseminate the story of Thomas Holloway, a truly remarkable Victorian.

I dedicate this book to Diane and her inspiration.

Introduction

Thomas Holloway was in some ways an unlikeable man: a self-seeking tycoon who made one fortune from unscrupulous advertising and another from stock-market speculation. But, in the end, he was also a philanthropist on a colossal scale. He left behind two extraordinary monuments: an asylum which looked like a Belgian town hall, and a ladies' college which conflated the imagery of half-a-dozen French châteaux.

How can the historian explain these things? It is one of the merits of John Elliott's book that he does not attempt to gloss over the paradoxes built into Holloway's career. Here was an educationalist with no education; a chemist ignorant of chemistry; a collector – or rather an accumulator – of paintings with little interest in art; a patron of building who chose as his architect a man then largely unknown and now almost completely forgotten. All these factors make for confusion. Perhaps the psychologist has some explaining to do as well. Holloway's buildings – like his fortune – were surely the expression of a remarkable ego. But it was an ego with little sense of direction. Having piled up his mountainous fortune, he seems to have been genuinely uncertain what to do with it. There were probably about two hundred Victorian millionaires in all; but only one who actually advertised for ways to give away his money. Still, as accidental beneficiaries of his largesse, we can today salute the spectacular profusion of Mr Thomas Holloway.

J Mordaunt Crook FBA
Emeritus Professor of Architectural History
University of London

Contents

The Men

The Victorian period was a time when economic and industrial change increased overall wealth, but also the extremes of wealth and poverty. So great were the changes, and so wide the divisions between those who had and those who had not, that while survival dominated the minds of one group, for others the problem became how to spend their ever-increasing fortune. The Great Exhibition, the museums of South Kensington and the proliferation of town halls, museums, libraries and art galleries throughout the nation attest this desire to spend at a governmental level, while numerous less dramatic works of munificence attest the contribution made by individuals.

Onto this stage walked many notable men, some concerned with the making of wealth, some with the spending of it, and some seeking an alternative society to the one which they thought brought good and bad in unequal measure. In politics Gladstone, Disraeli, and Lord Salisbury; in religion Temple, Blomfield, Wilberforce, Newman, Froude, Keble and many others; in science Stephenson, Bessemer, Brunel and Bell; in industry and commerce Armstrong, Minton, Wedgwood and the Rothschilds; in architecture Pugin, Scott, Street and Burges; in philosophy Mill, Ruskin, Carlyle and Bentham; in the arts and crafts Millais, Rossetti, William Morris and Burne Jones; on the stage Oscar Wilde and Bernard Shaw; and at the apex of society Prince Albert: all these collectively or individually grappled with the results of accelerating change.

To these *dramatis personae* must be added two other men, men who changed the society in which they lived; who left succeeding generations a memorial of their contribution, or to be precise, two memorials: buildings which by mid-1884 had cost £900,000,[1] and which continue to contribute to society more than one hundred years after they were first conceived. The two men were Thomas Holloway and William Crossland, and their buildings were the Holloway Sanatorium and The Royal Holloway College.

Thomas Holloway

Thomas Holloway (1800–83) was a man whose medicines were part of Victorian daily life, and whose advertising dominated both national and local newspapers. He spent the first sixty years of his life making a fortune, and the remainder engaged in the more difficult task of spending it.[2] He chose two projects which were for the benefit of the disadvantaged, those members of the middle classes suffering from mental disorders, and those women who wished to break with convention, by obtaining a degree of independence and individuality through a university style of education.

Details of Thomas Holloway's early life are somewhat obscure,[3] though it appears he was born in Devonport on 22 September 1800, the eldest of six children.[4] His parents were married in 1797[5] – Mary Chellew and Thomas Holloway senior[6] – his father allegedly being a navigating officer in the Navy,[7] then a baker in Devonport, and the landlord of two pubs, one in Devonport – the Robin Hood and Little John where Thomas junior was born – the other in Penzance, the Turk's Head where the family moved in 1811 and where Thomas spent most of his teenage years. Later Holloway senior became a grocer in Penzance before moving first to Dover and then to London.[8]

Opposite: Thomas Holloway.

Thomas junior was educated in Penzance, after which it seems possible he became apprenticed to a chemist, an appointment which may have provided the inspiration for his later business activities. In 1828 he left Penzance, moving to France where he lived at Dunkirk, and then at Roubaix. After about three years he moved to London as a secretary and interpreter, and by 1836 was established at 8 Wood Street where he traded as a merchant and foreign commercial agent, moving to 13 Broad Street Buildings shortly afterwards.

Holloway's first move to big business came through an association with Felix Albinolo, a leech-selling Italian, who, in 1837, sought Holloway's help with the marketing of an ointment – Albinolo's Ointment – though co-operation quickly turned to rivalry as the two competed for rights over the product. On 15 October 1837 Holloway placed an advertisement for 'Holloway's Ointment', and on 16 June 1838 another appeared in the *Town*, accompanied by a testimonial supposedly written by Mr Mayo, a surgeon at the Middlesex Hospital. Holloway's partner, the Italian leech seller, responded with an advertisement of his own in which he said that Mr Mayo's testimonial had been written about his ointment, and not that which Holloway was promoting. It seems that some form of compromise followed as Albinolo's name then replaced Holloway's, until in 1839 the Italian was gaoled for debt, and Holloway was left free to market the product as if it were his own. Holloway claimed that the ointment possessed a 'healing genius', though when analysed some years later it was found to consist of nothing more than yellow and white beeswax, resin, lanolin and olive oil.[9]

In 1863 Holloway provided a short account of his early business activities, an account that described the difficulties he faced.

> My task was very difficult and disheartening... I expended in one week the sum of £100 in advertising... and all I sold in that time was two small pots of ointment. In fact no person would then have accepted the medicine as a gift. I had to practise the most rigid economy and work most assiduously. By four o'clock in the morning I had generally commenced my day, not to cease till ten at night... So strong are the fetters of prejudice that my pills and ointment for a considerable time obtained little or no favours. But I did not suffer my energy to be readily daunted; I went on advertising, not only with determination, but judiciously and carefully, and in the end succeeded in creating for my preparations a limited reputation throughout the British Isles. This might have satisfied me at one time, but, as our desires increase with our success, I made up my mind to be content with nothing less than girdling the globe with depots of my remedies.[10]

Jane Holloway.

This overpowering desire for ever greater success meant that sales never kept pace with escalating advertising costs. *The Times* eventually foreclosed for non-payment of a debt, and Holloway was sent to Whitecross Street Debtors' Prison, gaining his freedom only when his mother provided £600. On his release Holloway was not deterred and started manufacturing pills as well as the ointment, the pills having a more complex formula which comprised aloes, rhubarb root, cinnamon, cardamon, ginger, saffron, Glauber's salt and potassium sulphate.[11] Such a combination of ingredients would have had a mildly laxative effect, though Holloway claimed the pills would cure almost anything – skin diseases, general paralysis, venereal disease and even cancer.

On 12 January 1840 Holloway married Jane Driver at St Mary Magdalene Bermondsey, Jane being the eldest daughter of John Driver, a Rotherhithe shipwright, and so started a partnership that was to dominate the years that followed. Almost immediately the business moved to better premises, to 244 the Strand,[12] a building which Holloway described as a 'Patent Medicines Warehouse', and from which he subsequently moved to 'Holloway House' at 533 Oxford Street. In 1848 Holloway travelled extensively in an attempt to create a worldwide market for his pills and ointments, visiting Belgium, the Netherlands, Germany and France.[13] In 1852 he visited the United States, and in 1853 undertook a second tour of Europe, visiting places as far apart as Rome, Dresden and St Petersburg.[14]

His diaries show that during these extensive overseas tours Holloway mixed business with pleasure, often accompanied by his wife. On 9 July 1848 he wrote:

> Poor Jane left Bruxelles with me this morning at half past eight and Antwerp by the Soho Steamer at 20 minutes past 11 in the morning. I was very dull and returned to Bruxelles at half past 3... When I arrived in my room at the Hotel without her where we had both been together only a few hours before I could hardly believe that she was no longer with me. God bless her she is one of the best of wives any man ever had.[15]

During 1848 Holloway visited Leiden Town Hall in Holland,[16] followed a little later by Strasbourg Cathedral,[17] a building which he declared was 'certainly the most splendid... I ever saw of this kind.'[18] However, it appears that he also had a penchant for gambling. Of Wiesbaden he wrote: 'arrived at town in the Evening went to the ? to see the Gambling on the Sunday'; of Hamburg 'There is much more Gambling going on here than at Wiesbaden'; while his diary entry for Liège recorded that 'There is a Salle for Gambling... but I do not think it at all the equal of Hamburg, Wiesbaden or Baden.' [19]

Throughout there was a concern for health, for his own health and for that of his wife, his diary recording regular weight checks,[20] and visits to the German health spas, facilities which he seemed to prefer to those at Matlock and Harrogate which he visited in 1864.[21]

Through agencies the Holloway products were sold in Asia, India, Africa and Australia; and the directions

> translated into almost every known tongue... [including] Chinese, Turkish, Armenian, Arabic, Sanskrit, and most of the vernaculars of India, and all the languages spoken on the European Continent.[22]

Holloway's annual advertising expenditure rose from £5,000 in 1842 to £10,000 in 1845, £20,000 in 1851, and £40,000 in 1863. He published an annual *Holloway's Almanac and Family Friend*, plus Holloway's *Abridged Medical Guide for the use of Missionaries and Others*, *Holloway's Atlas*, and a series of *Holloway's National Drawing Books*.[23] Much later the main competitors were Beecham's Pills and Eno's Fruit Salts, Eno's buying the Holloway business in 1930, and then itself being bought by Beecham in 1938.

In many ways the hard-faced Holloway is representative of the self-made man so much admired by the Victorians and of the self-confidence that pervaded the period. In 1877 he wrote a letter which he directed should be read to his employees once a year, so as to show 'what small beginnings may lead to, by ability, perseverance and industry'. Recalling his humble origins he wrote:

> Tomorrow, forty years ago, my advertisement appeared for the first time in three Sunday papers, the *Weekly Despatch*, the *Sunday Times*, and another paper, the name of which I have forgotten. I have, I believe, told you, that the first ointment I made was in my mother's saucepan, which held perhaps six quarts, an extra jump was in a long fish kettle, and after that her little copper, which would hold about forty pounds. The Pills were not started until two years after the ointment had come into existence. Hibberd, an old clerk, and myself used to take turn and turn about and go into the Cellar at 13 Broad Street Buildings, and make a few Pills with a small machine we had, and we used to put them into one of the little drawers of the desk, which was about six inches long, indeed, we used to count them. This was my first beginning... Now tomorrow, I wish you to call together in my back office, all the Clerks and porters, and read them the beginning of this paragraph, and then present each clerk a sovereign in gold, to the porters five shillings each in silver, and when you have done this, send

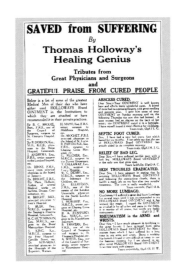

Tributes for Holloway's products.

for the Forewomen and all the girls, and read to them the extract, and then give to each of the girls two shillings and six pence, and to the Forewomen five shillings...You will tell them that my object in communicating to them my early beginning, is merely for their edification, as showing what small beginnings may lead to, by ability, perseverance, and industry.[24]

With affluence came an annual profit of £50,000, a country house at Sunninghill – Tittenhurst Park – a building Holloway acquired for £10,000; and one better known in modern times as the home of John Lennon and later Ringo Starr. Holloway now had wealth and status but – significantly for the future – no children.[25] With time he gradually passed more and more of the business operation to his brother-in-law – George Martin – while he set out in search of an even greater, and more immediately realisable fortune.

One of Holloway's first investments was a building development. It involved the purchase in 1869 of an adjacent Sunninghill property – Broomfield – and the transference of its art collection to his own house, before he replaced the building with a somewhat larger and more luxurious affair. If nothing else, this venture proved to Holloway that property development was not a route to riches, a more assured path being provided by the Stock Exchange, and trade in foreign stocks.

A brief examination of Holloway's letter book for the twelve months starting in August 1869 quickly shows how extensive his investment activities were. Some eighteen different stocks were traded, mostly those connected with overseas companies, and frequently those involving communications. For instance, he held investments in the South Austrian & Lombardo Venetian Railway Co, in the Eastern & Bengal Railway, in the Carnation Railway Co, in the New York Central Railroad, the Indian Tramway Co, the Telegraph Construction Co and the China Submarine Telegraph. In addition he held over £80,000 of Spanish, £10,000 of Argentinian, £25,000 of Italian, and over £78,000 of Turkish fixed interest bonds and stock.[26]

According to Anthony Harrison-Barbet, by 1 January 1876 Holloway's holdings were worth something over half a million pounds, with almost £230,000 in Turkish stock, £100,000 in Mexican Government loans, another £100,000 in Peruvian stock, and sizeable investments in the Great Indian Peninsular Railway, the Alabama & New Orleans & Texas Railway, the Alabama Great Southern Railway, the Atlantic & Great Western Leased Lines, and the Brazilian Submarine Telegraph.[27]

Holloway's letter book also makes it clear that he was playing the stock exchange rather than making long-term financial investments, a point well illustrated by a letter he wrote to his brokers – Knight & Greenwell – on 21 March 1870:

I note that you have bought back £25,000 of the 1865 Turks at 1/2 profit, and sold £15,000 of the same at about 1/2 net profit. If you can go on like this I think it will put some spirit into my brother. You have now to sell out the remaining £10,000 and then, (but not before), if you can again buy in at 1/2 profit clear of Commission, you may do so – and so on.[28]

Then in 1875 disaster struck; Jane Holloway died of bronchitis on 25 September and was buried in the churchyard of St Michael's at Sunninghill. Thomas withdrew from life, became somewhat reclusive, lost interest in living, and followed her on 26 December 1883. Both were commemorated by a memorial chapel designed by William Crossland and erected in 1888.

By June 1884 Holloway's personal fortunes had contributed almost £900,000 towards the two projects he had selected. Some £387,784 was spent on the College, £207,359 on the Sanatorium, and a further £300,000 set aside as an endowment.[29] Despite this generosity Holloway still left £596,335, a sum he bequeathed entirely to his sister-in-law, Mary Ann Driver.[30]

William Crossland

It was Holloway's business achievements, his consequential upward social progression, and his desire to leave a lasting memory of that success, that underlay his plan to build a Sanatorium and College, though it was through his architect – William Henry Crossland – that these dreams were converted into structural reality. Further, just as the Victorian concept of hierarchical mobility enabled Holloway to improve his social position, so also with Crossland, but in this case a rise followed by a decline; a rise from obscurity to social prominence, affluence and respectability, followed by a decline to obscurity and poverty.

William Henry Crossland (1834–1908) was born in Huddersfield,[31] and entered the architectural profession by becoming a pupil of that colossus of Victorian architecture, George Gilbert Scott.[32] Crossland worked under Scott and initially assisted with designs for the Akroydon Estate in Halifax, before starting in business on his own account.[33] His architectural practice was centred on Huddersfield, Halifax and Leeds,[34] a practice which was responsible for at least fifty-eight designs (a list of commissions is provided as an Appendix).

William Crossland.

From 1861 and his establishment in Halifax,[35] most of Crossland's ecclesiastical works were favourably reviewed in the *Ecclesiologist*. No less successful were his secular commissions, designs for buildings which included Rochdale Town Hall, two mansions – Rishworth Lodge near Halifax,[36] and Langley Hall at Huddersfield – and a host of commercial buildings in Huddersfield; commissions which largely arose from the patronage of two men, Edward Akroyd and John William Ramsden.

According to the *Builder* Edward Akroyd was 'a gentleman of well-known public spirit' who originated from Halifax, a town in which he had 'extensive factories.'[37] In 1847 Akroyd had commissioned an unknown architect to design Copley Mill, to which was added an estate of 'houses, for the accommodation of the workmen', a school and a library.[38] Then in 1863–5 Crossland added a church which was dedicated to St Stephen, a building which comprised a five-bay clerestoried nave, two aisles, and a seven-sided apsidal two-bay chancel all in the Early French Gothic style.

Elsewhere in Halifax Akroyd owned the Haley Hill Mills, manufactories which were built in 1836 and extended twenty years later. It was here that in the 1860s Akroyd attempted to recreate, in an improved form, the experiment in social housing he had conducted earlier at Copley Mill. In 1855 the *Builder* reported that Akroyd had purchased:

> a considerable plot of land, upon which he designed to build a small town, having, for its prime characteristics, beauty of architecture; a combination of all the improvements in arrangements evolved by the progress of sanitary science; and a town in which every inhabitant was his own landlord, living in his own freehold... [the] freeholders... [being] working men.[39]

In 1856 Akroyd commissioned G G Scott to design a church,[40] and then in 1859 he turned his energies towards the design of housing for his workers, and a 'new town [which would be built] in connection with a local society called the Halifax Permanent Benefit Building Society',[41] a town whose inhabitants would be that rare breed, the freehold manual labourer.

Akroyd commissioned Scott to prepare an initial design and Crossland to work up the detail, work starting in March 1861.[42] Throughout, the ethos conformed to Akroyd's version of the 'Old English notion of a village', an arrangement which had the 'squire and parson, as the head and the centre of all progress and good fellowship; then the tenant-farmers; and lastly, the working population.'[43] The site plan envisaged a regular arrangement of workers' houses gathered about a central reading room and clock tower, with allotments, villas and the church close by;[44] in short an idealized re-creation of medieval paternalism. However this was paternalism with a difference

Kirkgate Buildings.
Builder *6 January 1883, p 12.*

as at Akroydon individual achievement was also recorded, the initials of each householder being proudly displayed above his doorway.

A somewhat greater level of patronage was provided by Sir John William Ramsden, a man with extensive estates in the Huddersfield area, one who was educated at Eton and Cambridge, who later became a Deputy Lieutenant for the county of Inverness, a JP and High Sheriff for the West Riding of Yorkshire, and a politician of some standing.[45]

In 1878 Ramsden commissioned the Kirkgate Buildings in the centre of Huddersfield, buildings in the architectural style which had been adopted by the newly rich – the rising middle classes – a form of mongrel eclecticism that was half Gothic, half Classical, a style which looked to the French châteaux of the Loire for its inspiration. However, the Kirkgate Buildings were something more than that, they were also a precursor of the Holloway College, a northern opportunity for Crossland to try out much of the architectural decoration which was to find fuller expression at Egham a year later.

If the Kirkgate Buildings provided a Yorkshire precursor for the Holloway College, so Rochdale Town Hall in Lancashire had done much the same for the Sanatorium at Virginia Water. Rochdale was a product of the industrial revolution. Initially a centre for the woollen trade, it took to cotton in the mid-nineteenth century; the first cotton mill opened in 1850, and the town became a borough in 1855. The decision to build a town hall that was worthy of such success was made in 1858, though it was 1863 before a committee started examining other town halls, and specifically those at Leeds, Blackburn and Preston. In 1864 they recommended a competition be held amongst twenty-seven architects, the prize being the right to produce the designs for a town hall that would cost £20,000.[46] The winner was Crossland who proposed a building with a regular E-shaped plan, an irregular silhouette, and a style that the *Builder* described as being 'of a similar character to that which obtained in England at the end of the fourteenth century'. More accurately it was a fusion of French, Flemish and English precedents.[47]

The plan was dominated by a seven-bay central range, while there were two side ranges, one housing the Council offices and library, and the other accommodating the Courts, the Police and the Fire Brigade, the whole being terminated by a clock tower topped with an octagonal lantern. The ground floor of the central range contained the Council Chamber, and in 1865 a three-bay vaulted and polychromed exchange was added, with the interior supported on marble columns. At the rear a magnificent groined staircase – a precursor to what would follow at Virginia Water – gave access to the floor above and a seven-bay pseudo-medieval hall, complete with a hammerbeam roof and elaborate decoration which glorified past and present monarchs, and somewhat prophetically, the sealing of the Magna Carta at Runnymede. Elsewhere, decoration in the Council Chamber glorified the cotton trade and the contribution made by mechanisers like Samuel Crompton, John Kay, Edmund Cartwright and James Hargreaves.[48] Work clearing the site started in 1864; the foundation stone was laid on 31 March 1866, and the completed building opened on 27 September 1871, by which time the estimated cost of £20,000 had escalated to £154,755.[49] The lantern was burnt down in 1883, and the tower was rebuilt in 1887 to somewhat different designs by Alfred Waterhouse.[50]

Crossland married Lavinia Cardwell in 1859,[51] and the following year their daughter was born in Halifax.[52] In 1867 he achieved a degree of professional respectability, becoming a fellow of the Royal Institute of British Architects, though by the 1870s he had shifted his allegiance from Yorkshire to London, his patronage from Akroyd and Ramsden to Thomas Holloway, and his style from Gothic to the Renaissance.

Crossland had also shifted his love from his wife Lavinia to an actress eighteen years his junior – Eliza Ruth Hatt. By 1870 this affair had found its first physical expression through the birth of an illegitimate son,[53] and though Crossland still lived near Regent's Park with his wife and daughter,[54] the financial effects of this dual life were starting to have a dramatic effect. In 1876 Holloway refused Crossland's request for additional funds as he had already received £7,500 for

Rochdale Town Hall.
Builder *24 November 1866, p 869.*

his work on the Sanatorium plus a £500 advance towards future work on the College, though in 1877 Holloway recorded how he had given Crossland £1,000 'as he stated that he has no money whatever left', despite having been paid £9,500, a sum which was £1,800 more than the total to which he was entitled.[55]

Four years later life became somewhat simpler. Crossland's wife died at Boulogne in 1879,[56] and he 'had a bungalow built... [on the college site where he] went into residence' with the actress,[57] a lady who by then had given birth to two other sons;[58] and so commenced a brief episode 'of uninterrupted interest and pleasure.'[59]

With time, and less complicated financial family arrangements, came affluence and a house in Bloomsbury;[60] but success mixed with little happiness. Crossland's eldest son died in 1886, to be followed in 1892 by his lover Eliza Ruth Hatt, and in 1900 by his daughter Maud.[61] All three were buried at Highgate alongside his wife Lavinia. Progressively Crossland retreated into his own world, slipping from prominence to obscurity, and from wealth to poverty. His last major commission appears to have been for the Holloway Memorial Chapel at Sunninghill (1888), though he was retained by the college until 1900, designing a swimming pool in 1893.[62] His name disappears from the RIBA records in the mid-1890s.[63] However the end was slow in coming; his small fortune leaked away, and he died of a stroke in a Camden Town lodging house during 1908 with a worldly wealth of just £29.[64]

Crossland Memorial at Highgate Cemetery. Builder 1882, p 136.

Opposite: Rochdale Town Hall. Builder 12 February 1876, p 146.

Notes

1   This is equivalent to about £40m in current values.

2   See Caroline Bingham, 'The Founder and the Founding of the Royal Holloway College', in M Moore (ed), *Centenary Lectures*, Egham 1988, p 1.

3   For a detailed account see A Harrison-Barbet, *Thomas Holloway: Victorian Philanthropist*, Egham 1993.

4   These were Mary Jane (1805), Henry (1807), Caroline (1812), Matilda (1813) and Emma (1821).

5   At Falmouth on 6 November 1797.

6   She was the daughter of a Cornish farmer. His origins are unknown.

7   It is claimed that he served on HMS *Ganges* and took part in the Battle of Ushant though Richard Williams tells me that searches of the crew lists of HMS *Ganges* have failed to find any Holloway listed.

8   Holloway senior died aged 72 on 13 April 1836, his address at that time being 4 Greyhound Place, Dun Cow Road, Old Street, London. His wife died on 26 March 1843 when she was 67 and living above her son's 'Patent Medicines Warehouse' at 244 Strand, London.

9   See Caroline Bingham, *The History of the Royal Holloway College 1886–1986*, Egham 1987, p 274.

10 See Caroline Bingham, 'The Founder and the Founding of the Royal Holloway College', in M Moore (ed), *Centenary Lectures*, Egham 1988, pp 6–7.

11 See Caroline Bingham, *The History of the Royal Holloway College 1886–1986*, Egham 1987, p 275.

12 In 1841.

13 See Holloway's 1848 diary at the Surrey History Centre.

14 See transcript of Holloway's 1853 diary at the Surrey History Centre.

15 See 1848 diary at Surrey History Centre.

16 On 3 June 1848.

17 On 13 September 1848.

18 Ibid.

19 Ibid. He visited Wiesbaden on 3rd September, Hamburg on 7th and Liège on 24th.

20 His 1848 diary records a series of weight checks which were made between 1855 and 1866, and where his weight varied between 12 stone and 13 stone 10 lbs, while Jane was 11 stone 3 lbs in 1855 and 13 stone 2 lbs in 1864.

21 He visited one at Boppart in 1848 and recorded that he had made an arrangement there with Dr Herbert Mayo from London - see 1848 diary at Surrey History Centre. For details of his visits to Matlock and Harrogate see 1864 diary.

22 Caroline Bingham, 'The Founder and the Founding of the Royal Holloway College', in M Moore (ed), *Centenary Lectures*, Egham 1988, pp 9–10.

23 Caroline Bingham, *The History of the Royal Holloway College 1886–1986*, Egham 1987, p 27.

24 Ibid pp 5–6.

25 See *The Story of Thomas Holloway (1800–1883)*, Glasgow 1933, pp 11–12 & 20.

26 See letter book August 1869 to July 1870 at Surrey History Centre. The investments were £80,000 in Spanish 1869 stock, £10,000 in Argentinian 1868 6% bonds, £17,500 in Turkish 1858 and over £78,000 in Turkish 1865 stock, plus £25,000 in 5% Italian stock.

27 A Harrison-Barbet, *Thomas Holloway: Victorian Philanthropist*, St Austell 1990, p 19.

28 See letter book August 1869 to July 1870 at Surrey History Centre.

29 A memo book held by the Surrey History Centre records these figures, while also indicating that a further £5,000 had been set aside for expected future bills making a total spend of £900,143.

30 See will at Somerset House.

31 See 1891 census RG12 208 f135.

32 Scott was one of the most prolific Victorian architects, perhaps his most remembered design being the Albert Memorial (1864–8). Crossland's pupilship is mentioned by the *Builder* in its article on Akroydon dated 14 February 1863 p 110 and by Akroyd in his 1862 publication *On Improved Dwellings for the Working Classes*.

33 He started in business on his own about 1860. For further information on Crossland see the papers deposited at the RIBA by Mr Edward Law.

34 He was at Harrison Road, Halifax with a residence at 6 Trinity Place in 1861 and 1863–4. By 1864 he had an office at 17 Albion Street, Leeds, in 1866 he was recorded at 23 Corn Exchange Gallery, Leeds with a residence at East House, Roundhay, while in 1869 and 1870 his business address is recorded as at 25 Park Square, Leeds.

35 In 1861 the *Ecclesiologist* noted that Crossland was 'a young architect [who has] lately settled in Halifax' – *Ecclesiologist* 1861, p 197.

36 This was commissioned by Captain Henry Saville the illegitimate son of the 8th Earl of Scarborough.

37 *Builder* 14 February 1863, p 109. The factories were worsted mills. He was a JP, a Lieutenant Colonel in the 4th West Yorkshire Rifle Volunteers, MP for Huddersfield 1857–9, and then for Halifax 1865–74.

38 The school was added in 1849, the library in 1850 and the estate completed by 1853.

39 *Builder* 14 February 1863, p 109.

40 All Souls, Haley Hill (1856–9).

41 *Builder* 14 February 1863, p 109.

42 The town was called Akroydon and is now known as Boothtown. There were several different types of house, each having a basement and two floors above, plus two or three bedrooms in addition to a kitchen and living room. The cheapest house cost £130, with more expensive versions at £190, £210 and £300.

43 *Builder* 14 February 1863, p 109.

44 The plan was illustrated in the *Builder* on 14 February 1863. The financial arrangements required the owners to make a deposit of one quarter of the cost, though Akroyd arranged for this to be included in the monthly mortgage payments which were spread over twelve years, and provided by the Halifax Permanent Benefit Building Society, Akroyd acting as the guarantor.

45 He was the MP for Taunton (1853–7), for Hythe (1857–9), the West Riding (1859–65), Monmouth (1868–74), the eastern division of the West Riding (1880–6) and Under Secretary for War (1857–8).

46 See L J Whitaker, *W H Crossland: His Architectural Development*, MA dissertation Manchester University 1984, p 122.

47 *Builder* 24 November 1866, p 867.

48 Samuel Crompton invented the spinning mule (1785), James Hargreaves the spinning jenny (1764-7), Edmund Cartwright designed the power loom (1785) and John Kay the flying shuttle (1733).

49 See L J Whitaker, *W H Crossland: His Architectural Development*, MA dissertation Manchester University 1984, p 146.

50 The tower originally formed a corner of the building while the one designed by Waterhouse was built slightly apart from the main structure although connected to it by a first floor passage which also acted as a porte cochère. The rebuilt tower was also somewhat shorter than the one designed by Crossland.

51 At the St Pancras Old Church in London on 1 October 1859.

52 The family lived at 6 Trinity Place, Halifax – see 1861 census RG9 3283 f49 p 10.

53   Benjamin Tilley Hatt (born 1870).

54   At 12 Park Village West, Albany Street – see the 1871 census RG 10 203 f6 p 5.

55   Crossland received 6% commission for his work at the Sanatorium and 5% for the College. See letter dated 3 August 1877 at Surrey History Centre. See also the Sanatorium Purchase Ledger at Surrey History Centre.

56   She was buried at Highgate Cemetery in plot 23297. Crossland designed a memorial which was illustrated in the *Builder* of 1882, vol 1, p 136.

57   See 1881 census RG 11 1322 f35 p29.

58   William Henry Crossland Hatt and Cecil Henry Crossland Hatt (born 1877).

59   W Crossland, 'The Royal Holloway College' in *RIBA Transactions* 1887, p 145.

60   46 Upper Bedford Place, where in 1891 he lived with Eliza Ruth, their son Cecil Henry and two servants – see 1891 census RG12 208 f135.

61   She was Maud Helen Lart who was buried on 12 March 1900.

62   See Jeannie Chapel, *Victorian Taste*, Egham 1982, p 12.

63   He disappeared from the RIBA records in 1894–5 when he was living at 18 Great George Street, Westminster.

64   He died on 14 November 1908 and was not buried in the Highgate Cemetery plot despite a specific request in his will. His estate was worth £29/2/9d.

The Sanatorium

In 1808 an Act of Parliament known as Wynn's Act permitted county justices to build asylums at public expense, and the Lunacy Act of 1845 made such provision mandatory. Thus began an era of asylum building. However, for the upper and middle classes the seeds of change had occurred much earlier, having their origins in the heightened interest aroused by the madness of George III. In 1808 there were twenty-eight private asylums in England and Wales, and this number was to grow to thirty-eight in 1815, fifty-eight in 1825, and one hundred in 1844 before the mandatory nature of the 1845 act shifted the emphasis from private to State provision, and so encouraged a gradual decline in private institutions.[1]

However, before 1845 the needs of those who were economically less fortunate were not ignored. Some seventeen public pauper asylums were built between 1808 and 1846 – the earliest at Bedford, Nottingham and Norwich[2] – and a further seventeen were added between 1847 and 1853. A growing interest in insanity as a separate medical condition, plus the growth in asylums, meant that by 1859 there were 15,842 pauper patients in forty county and borough asylums, plus another 7,686 mentally deranged patients in workhouses, while by 1884 the numbers of patients had risen to 45,464 and the number of asylums to sixty-three.[3]

The preferred asylum plan was one which utilised a central range supported by subordinate side ranges, one side range providing accommodation for male patients while the other catered for females. The emphasis in all early establishments was on security, the nearest architectural analogy being a prison. In 1847 Dr J Conolly attempted to change this, his book on *The Construction and Government of Lunatic Asylums* suggesting that:

> the external aspect of an asylum should be more cheerful than imposing, more resembling a well-built hospital than a place of seclusion or imprisonment. It should be surrounded by gardens, or a farm.[4]

Progressively regimes were lightened, patients were allowed more freedom, the corridors became wider and bay windows were introduced to enliven both the interior plan and the façade. By 1856 the Commissioners in Lunacy were differentiating between those who were chronically insane and those who would be accommodated in 'asylums primarily for... treatment and relief', namely a differentiation between those who were incurable and those who were confidently expected to recover, and where the cost was not of primary importance.[5]

By 1870 the process of patient classification had been expanded in such a way that asylum planning anticipated that 15% of patients would be sick, and 20% acute, leaving the vast majority as those whose condition could be improved or cured if treated correctly. Meanwhile the regime had been eased still further, an acre of recreational ground was required for each patient, as was easy access to good transport facilities so as to encourage visits, plus mains gas and a water supply that would guarantee forty gallons a day for each patient.[6]

Simultaneously the effects of colour on a deranged mind were being studied on the Continent, and the elaborate decoration of wall surfaces was increasingly advocated; though in Britain there was always a clash between those who emphasised the possibilities of recovery and tended to disregard cost, and those who made cost the primary objective, and who as late as 1911 declared that 'all superfluous decoration must be avoided'.[7]

The Victorian period was of course one of great economic and social change. In less than the space of one man's lifetime the advance of industrialization meant that national income almost

Opposite:The Sanatorium at Virginia Water.

1. General View from the Drive.—2. The Recreation Hall.—3. The Dining Hall.—4. A Patient's Room.—5. Entrance Hall and Staircase.

THE HOLLOWAY COLLEGE AND SANATORIUM AT VIRGINIA WATER

tripled,[8] and the population increased by 55%.[9] Three Reform Acts extended the franchise,[10] shifting the basis of power away from a landed aristocracy, and towards an entrepreneurial middle class, such that by 1885 two out of three English males were able to vote compared with one in five in 1831.[11] This process of industrialization shifted the basis of power and wealth away from the possession of land to the control of productive capital, and in the process created a middle class eager to display their newly found economic power.

In 1859 a Parliamentary Select Committee examined the care of the insane, with Lord Shaftesbury as one of the chief witnesses. Shaftesbury claimed that while pauper asylums catered for the poorer classes and private establishments for the wealthy, there was no real provision for the middle classes. On 19 April 1861 Holloway attended a public meeting where Lord Shaftesbury attempted to raise £5,000 for a middle-class asylum, and while there was no immediate impact, in 1864 Holloway's solicitor informed Lord Shaftesbury that 'a gentleman possessed of nearly a quarter of a million' was interested in such a project, though again nothing happened despite a meeting between Shaftesbury and Holloway on 25 May.[12]

By 1871 Holloway was rich, famous, childless, elderly and as he told Murray Lindsay of the renowned asylum at Hanwell, 'desirous... of building... [an institution] for the lower Middle Classes whose means may be very small',[13] an establishment that would 'contain about 200 patients'. Holloway wanted the asylum to be a model which could be copied, as his travels had taught him that scarcely any existing asylum building he had seen was worthy of imitation because 'the class of architects to whom such buildings have been entrusted are not men possessed of great ability'.[14]

In September 1871 Holloway sought the advice of E W Pugin.[15] In a letter which congratulated Pugin on a critique he had written for *The Times*,[16] Holloway announced that he intended building an asylum for two hundred paying patients, and that in addition to the land, he would 'have no objection to spend[ing] £40,000 or more on the Building'.[17] The intended style would be 'the purest Italian', and the 'river frontage of Somerset House shall so far as practical serve as a model'.[18] The reply has not survived, though Holloway cited Pugin's words in another letter he wrote later that month, a letter in which he referred to 'the suggestion which a great man has made to me', a suggestion that 'Instead of an Italian Building I would recommend you to adopt the grand old Flemish Style of Brick Building', a structure which Holloway thought must allude 'to Gothic & perhaps to the Cloth Hall... at "Ypres" a town in Belgium'.[19]

Having determined the style, the main unresolved matters were who would produce the designs, and to what set of requirements would the architect work. In December 1871 Holloway sought advice on the required arrangement of rooms from Dr Yellowlees, the medical superintendent of the Bridgend Asylum, as architects 'know but little the requirements',[20] and a few months later he asked Professor Donaldson to provide a list of suitable architects who would be invited to enter a limited competition.

A result of these deliberations was the publication in 1872 of *Suggestions for A Proposed Lunatic Asylum*, though unlike the county asylums the 'Building is not intended for Pauper Patients; but for Persons of the reduced middle class, who will pay a moderate fixed sum for their support.'[21] Those whom the *Globe* described as 'in the incipient stage of mental protuberance',[22] and whom the *Builder* subsequently described as:

> the unfortunate student who has overdone 'cramming' for some public examination,-for the overworked barrister or clergyman,– [and] for those whose minds are 'filled with illusions' on account of domestic troubles or bereavements.[23]

The requirement was that the building should hold two hundred patients, none of whom were to be epileptic, paralytic or dirty, the design being 'in the style of the Geometrical period of Gothic

Opposite: The Sanatorium at Virginia Water. The Graphic *22 October 1881.*

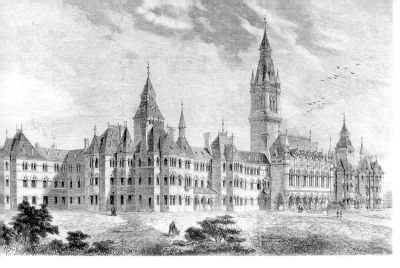

Architecture of which the Cloth Hall at Ypres is an excellent Continental example'. There should be 'A single tower of moderate height', plus 'A noble Hall... with a Stage, suitable for recreation, or for religious services', though all 'Exuberance of ornament [was] to be strictly avoided', as the cost should not exceed £40,000, on which commission would be paid at the rate of 5%.[24]

The competition resulted in thirteen entries all of which were examined for their architectural merit by Professor Donaldson and T H Wyatt,[25] and for their medical provision by Dr Yellowlees and Dr Lockhart Robertson. Amongst the designs was one produced by a triumvirate of architects called Crossland, Salomons & Jones,[26] a combination which according to Crossland arose from 'an interview which I had with Mr Holloway at his place of business, after which I did not feel inclined to go single-handed into this competition, and [so] I sought the assistance of... John Philpott-Jones, of Whitehall Place, in whose hands I practically left the working-out of the design.'[27] Then in July 1872 Holloway asked the *Builder* to publish the results of the Donaldson and Wyatt adjudication, a process which had selected the design produced by Crossland and his associates. The adjudicators reported:

> We must state that although there is considerable merit and taste displayed in the several projects, and evidence of a great amount of time and care having been bestowed upon the preparation of the drawings, yet there is not one of the designs which would not require more or less modification of plan and general arrangement ere it could be carried into execution for practical working, consequently we have selected that one as first which, with the least alteration and no sacrifice of its own individual character, would, we believe, be the most suited to your purpose, and the least costly.[28]

In 1872 the *Builder* published an elevational drawing, a ground floor plan and a review, reporting that 'The buildings are to be of red bricks, with stone arches and string-courses'. The plan would comprise a large central range with separate male and female accommodation gathered around quadrangles on either side, while various domestic elements were to be gathered into a further range at the north-eastern corner. A large central tower and spire would dominate the silhouette, and would be supported by shorter and dumpier towers, one above the male accommodation and the other above the female wing, while the roofs and exterior façades were to be an exercise in variety and asymmetry.

According to the *Builder* 'The building... [would consist] of three stories; the upper story being exclusively devoted to sleeping accommodation', the 'accommodation for the male and female patients... [being] kept distant on either side of the central entrance and great hall'. The grand entrance and staircase was intended only to be used 'for visitors on state occasions', and would lead to:

> A large hall... [which would be] provided central to both sides, having service-rooms and lifts from the kitchen, so as to serve for public dinners if required... The hall... [being] fitted with a platform at the end, and a gallery... which may be made available for an orchestra.[29]

In the basement there would be 'a Turkish bath, hot air and vapour bath',[30] while on the ground floor there would be a 'library for male, [and] also [a] separate one for female patients'.[31] Stylistically the central hall was loosely modelled on the Cloth Hall at Ypres, though the style of the remainder of the structure could be more properly described as early French Renaissance, and combined Italian, French and Belgian Gothic.[32]

The first brick was laid by Jane Holloway in June 1873, the second by Holloway himself, though within two years the proposed internal arrangements were modified, the plan being made E-shaped and becoming dominated by the central range, while many of the rooms were interconnected and the axial corridors removed.[33] Because of Holloway's intervention, Portland stone dressings were substituted for the more expensive cut and moulded bricks,[34] the central hall and tower were made to resemble more closely the Cloth Hall at Ypres; and the tower was reduced in height and simplified.[35] In 1875 the triumvirate of Crossland, Salomons and Jones broke up, Jones dying and Salomons losing interest, leaving Crossland to exhibit the amended design at the Royal Academy, and to supervise construction with his brother James.[36]

Holloway made regular visits to the site, and as his letter book for 1874–5 reveals, his influence was substantial. In October 1874 he wrote to Crossland about the windows, suggesting it would not 'suit our purpose to follow the Hanwell arrangement', instead suggesting a visit to Brentwood in search of precedents as:

the fastening of these windows appears to me, to be of the utmost importance, for if you have not got the right kind of thing, the ingenuity of a madman will enable him to open it, and so get out and break his neck.[37]

Then in November Holloway suggested changes to the roofs of the hall and the dining room which included the addition of roof turrets, an arrangement with 'windows in each of its octagonal parts' to make it a 'better feature', and one not unlike 'that [which] I admired at Chambord.'[38]

Throughout the period of construction there was an unending search for ideas and inspiration.[39] Holloway's aim was to 'give to the Country a Model place', an objective which could not be achieved 'in your office or mine', instead the need was to go out and see what others were doing 'so as to avoid all kinds of mistakes.'[40] Holloway suggested Crossland look for ideas at an asylum in Perth,[41] that he seek inspiration for decorating the staircase by driving around a variety of hotels and clubs, such a feature being recognised as important 'In New York' where 'Staircase making... [was] a business of itself.'[42] For Holloway the prize of such research was immense, and he told Crossland 'You are sowing the seed now to reap hereafter a golden harvest', and one which would mean that if people 'wish to see a Model place, they must go to St Anne's Heath [and] to the Sanatorium built by Mr Wm Crossland.'[43]

In 1877 the *Builder* reported that the Sanatorium was 'now approaching completion', though the cost had escalated to £150,000. Then almost instantly disaster struck. The building was refused a licence as legislation now required that 'all rooms occupied by lunatics should open into a corridor from which a staircase should lead directly to the outside'.[44] According to Crossland:

Dr Yellowlees and Mr Jones had planned a building on altogether different principles; and when the commissioners were asked to pass the building, they, acting under new rules, refused. The whole internal arrangements had consequently to be changed, and they are now practically the same as originally designed by Mr Jones and myself.[45]

The axial corridors were restored and additional staircases added, leaving a building which would accommodate three hundred patients[46] though it was not opened until 1885 when the Prince and Princess of Wales performed the ceremony on 15 June.[47] The cost by then had risen to a massive £207,359,[48] a sum equivalent to about £10m today.

Opposite

Top: Builder *24 August 1872, p 667.*

Centre: Builder *17 July 1875, p 645.*

Bottom: Builder *14 July 1877, p 712–3.*

In 1882 the *Builder* reported that 'although [the Sanatorium had been] erected for the benefit of those who are suffering from mental disorders, it is not intended to be devoted to the uses of an ordinary asylum for the insane', Holloway having attached certain rules 'which are novel', and which required that:

> no patient will be allowed to remain an inmate of the institution for a longer period than twelve months; no patient will be received whose case is considered hopeless; no patient will be allowed to enter the Sanatorium after having been once discharged; and the patients received are to be of the middle class.[49]

Dining Hall.

The reviewer for the *Builder* reported that the site was 'remarkably picturesque', 'surrounded by twenty-two acres of freehold land', yet also convenient, being adjacent to Virginia Water railway station. The great 'Ypres type [tower was], 145 ft. high', the wings of the building 'broken up by lofty crow-stepped gables, so as to form a series of separate groups of houses, yet all [was] united together by the string and horizontal members carried over the whole design without any break.'[50] Inside 'Costly pictures and excellent engravings... [had been] hung on all sides of the numerous day-rooms throughout the building',[51] while outside the grounds were laid out with a cricket ground, pavilion, tennis courts and bowling green.

There was 'a remarkably handsome dining-hall' which had an open timber roof, and walls which were 'entirely covered with decorative paintings and arabesques.'[52] The surfaces of the entrance hall and main staircase were 'covered with painted decorations presenting a most sumptuous appearance. Such a combination of rich colouring and gilding... [was] not to be found in any modern building in this country, except the House of Lords.' The purpose of such a lavish interior was well summarized by the *Tipperary Free Press*, which in 1877 reported that the decoration 'will be made to contribute to the system of cure by "distraction" according to the French method',[53] while the *Graphic* reported that 'Cold grey columns and walls, even if enlivened by sculpture, would, it was thought, sit heavily on a mind diseased.'[54]

Great Hall.

The recreation hall was eighty feet long by forty feet wide and sixty feet high, topped by an immense hammer beam roof, with three hundred and thirty-eight panels each gilded and decorated with painted motifs,[55] while the walls were ablaze with 'decorative painting, [and] gilding', with shamrocks and thistles, with griffons, ravens, dogs, owls, hares and storks, plus a floral frieze, and depictions of saints.[56] If all this was too romantic and heavenly the lower part of the walls would provide earthly exemplars to emulate, with portraits of distinguished individuals,[57] depictions which included Queen Victoria, Prince Albert, the Prince and Princess of Wales, the Duke of Marlborough, Alfred the Great, Wellington, Raleigh, Nelson, Shakespeare, Cromwell, Disraeli, Gladstone, Francis Bacon and Isaac Newton, plus Thomas and Jane Holloway.[58] According to the *Globe* this social elevation of Holloway and his wife was reinforced by a 'statue of the founder [which] stands on a black temporary pedestal' in the centre of the hall, while 'a monogram of his initials forms the centre of the panels in the ceilings'.[59] More accurately they could have reported that the Holloway initials and their adopted coats of arms were repeated over and over again in various parts of the building lest anyone should forget whose munificence and success was responsible for such a grand construction.

Contemporary opinions varied. *The Times* reported that 'Indeed it is not too much to say that the place is more than comfortable – it is luxurious'.[60] The *Builder* was no less impressed, describing the Sanatorium as a 'sumptuously decorated palace', one that was 'a bold experiment in... design', a structure which 'at first sight appears to be a work of the fourteenth-century style', though one which upon more careful examination will be seen to contain elements from 'the thirteenth and fifteenth century', a mixture for which there was 'no direct authority', but one which seemed 'to offer a suggestion for the formation of a new style, one which would be representative of the Victorian age.[61]

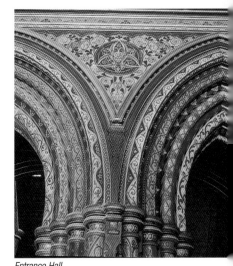
Entrance Hall.
Opposite: The Sanatorium at Virginia Water.

The *Globe* was less enthusiastic reporting that 'The "Holloway Sanatorium" is a building upon whose architectural merits, no doubt, opinions will differ considerably', and that while the building was 'decidedly striking and effective in design', it suffered from 'a certain degree of bareness and angularity in appearance'.[62]

The *Graphic* published a composite illustration, and commented that the 'aim of the architect has evidently been to unite the three pure Gothic styles', a mixture which 'might lead the way to the introduction of a new style of Gothic Architecture'.[63] Perhaps more importantly Holloway himself was pleased, telling Crossland that the building 'will immortalize you', and especially:

> Your magnificent [recreation] Room and its height – your Dining room, your Billiard room – Your magnificent terrace, running the whole length of the Building, 40 ft wide, which will be reached by handsome flights of steps – Speak of your Entrance Hall & Grand Staircase ? that the grounds will be equal to those of the Crystal Palace.[64]

A chapel was added in 1882 after a recommendation by the Commissioners in Lunacy, the materials echoing the sanatorium with red brick and Portland stone, though the style had shifted from an eclectic mixture of north European precedents to flamboyant French Gothic. The building was dominated by a western end which displayed stepped gables, a traceried rose window, and flanking octagonal towers with ogee cupolas. The plan comprised a four-bay nave plus a three-sided apsidal east end, the whole being connected to the main sanatorium buildings by a covered corridor.[65] Inside, the apsidal chancel was elevated from the nave and terminated by a stone altarpiece which commemorated Christ in Majesty and the four evangelists.

At the time that Holloway planned his sanatorium the nearest comparable establishment was the Hospital for the insane which had been built at Cotton Hill near Stafford around 1854,[66] an establishment 'intended for the upper and middle portions of society'.[67] At Cotton Hill there were separate entrances for the two classes and accommodation for one hundred and fifty, but without any of the lavishness which was such a feature at Virginia Water, a difference which explains why the Holloway Sanatorium cost £207,359 while that at Cotton Hill was built for just £29,000.[68]

As was suggested in the preceding chapter the precedent for the Holloway Sanatorium was Rochdale Town Hall, a building which Crossland had designed some eight years earlier, and one which also looked to Ypres for its inspiration. Similarities between Rochdale Town Hall and the Sanatorium are striking, not only in the façade and roof line, not only in the elaborate entrance stairway and great hall, but also in the iconographical decoration which was used in both buildings. At both, the emphasis was on success and heritage, the difference being that at Rochdale the focus was on civic and collaborative achievement, while at Virginia Water it was the success and status of individuals, and in particular the commercial success of Thomas and Jane Holloway and their world famous potions.

In 1871 a board of trustees was established to manage the Sanatorium,[69] the organization registering as a charity in 1889.[70] Later the complex passed to the Health Service where it remained, operating as a mental hospital until December 1981 when medical advances, and a changed attitude towards mental illness made it redundant. There followed a period when various developers speculated, a period when, according to the Victorian Society, the Sanatorium was 'a miserable example of how conservation legislation can fail to protect a Grade I listed building'.[71] Then in 1994 Octagon Developments acquired the site, and in exchange for restoring the main structure were given permission to develop the grounds and to convert the side wings of the original building into three-storey town houses. Under this scheme the recreation hall, staircase and entrance hall were restored as public areas, the dining hall became a swimming pool *(photo opposite),* and the chapel became a recreation hall.

Great Hall, Dining Hall and Chapel.

Opposite: The Dining Hall today.

Photos held by Surrey History Centre.

Notes

1   There were eighty-eight private asylums in 1870. See L J Whitaker, *W H Crossland: His Architectural Development*, MA Thesis Manchester University 1984, p 184.

2   See J Taylor, *Hospital & Asylum Architecture in England 1840–1914*, London 1991, pp 133–4.

3   By 1914 there were 101,538 patients in ninety-seven County and Borough asylums, plus a further 7,299 in five Metropolitan institutions. See J Taylor, *Hospital & Asylum Architecture in England 1840–1914*, London 1991, pp 138, 141, 148 & 155. For a comprehensive account of the development of asylums see Harriet Richardson (ed), *English Hospitals 1660–1949: A Survey of their Architecture and Design*, Swindon: Royal Commission on the Historical Monuments of England, 1998, pp 154–181

4   Ibid, p 135.

5   Ibid, pp 135 & 141.

6   L J Whitaker, *W H Crossland: His Architectural Development*, MA Dissertation Manchester University 1984, p 186.

7   J Taylor, *Hospital & Asylum Architecture in England 1840–1914*, London 1991, pp 154 & 139.

8   It was £636m in 1855 and had risen to £1,750m by 1900 – see C Cook & J Stevenson, The *Longman Handbook of Modern British History 1714–1987*, Harlow 1988, p 216.

9   For England, Wales and Ireland it increased from 26.7m in 1841 to 41.5m in 1901 – Ibid, pp 110–1.

10 These were the Reform Act of 1832, and the Representation of the People Acts of 1867 and 1884.

11 The percentage of all adults able to vote rose from just 5% of the population in 1831 to 28.5% in 1884 – see C Cook & J Stevenson, *The Longman Handbook of Modern British History 1714–1987*, Harlow 1988, p 68.

12 Caroline Bingham, 'Founder and Founding', in M Moore (ed), *Centenary Lectures*, Egham 1988, p 12.

13 Letter dated 21 February 1871 at Surrey History Centre.

14 He was much involved with the asylums at Hanwell, Colney Heath and Bridgend – see letter book at Surrey History Centre.

15 The son and successor of A W N Pugin.

16 The issue of 13 September.

17 The charges were to be 15/- and 20/- a week. Letter dated 16 September 1871 at Surrey History Centre.

18 Ibid.

19 Letter to Alfred Smith dated 24 September 1871 in Surrey History Centre. Clearly Holloway had never seen the Cloth Hall at Ypres as he promptly wrote to Pugin asking if he 'could see a print of this celebrated Building as I should much like to study it' – letter Holloway to Pugin 26 September 1871 in Surrey History Centre.

20 Letter dated 13 December 1871 in Surrey History Centre. He also sought the advice of Dr Lockhart Robertson – see *Builder* 27 July 1872, p 589.

21 *Builder* 7 January 1882, p 23.

22 *Globe* 13 July 1881.

23 *Builder* 7 January 1882, p 23.

24 Held by Surrey History Centre.

25 Letter Donaldson to Crossland dated 18 March 1872 in Surrey History Centre. The thirteen were T H Watson, Alfred Smith, Thomas C Hine, R Phéné Spiers, Edward W Godwin, T Roger Smith, J S Quilter, J P Seddon, Wm Knight, John Norton, F & H Francis, R Brandon, W H Crossland. Wyatt was the architect to the Lunacy Commissioners.

26 Edward Salomons (1827–1906) and John Philpot Jones (?–1875). Second prize was awarded to Alfred Smith, while a £50 award was given to T R Smith, R P Spiers, J P Seddon, E W Godwin, T H Watson and F & H Francis. See *Builder* 3 August 1872, p 609.

27 W H Crossland, 'The Royal Holloway College' in *RIBA Transactions* 1887, p 142.

28 *Builder* 27 July 1872, p 589.

29 *Builder* 31 March 1883, p 412.

30 The Turkish baths had marble seats and wall linings, while a shampooing room had a marble basin and pedestal. See *Builder* 31 March 1883, p 412.

31 *Builder* 24 August 1872, p 665.

32 See J M Crook, 'Holloway's Architect and Château' in M Moore (ed), *Centenary Lectures*, Egham 1988, pp 30 & 39.

33 See L J Whitaker, *W H Crossland: His Architectural Development*, Manchester University MA dissertation 1984, p 198.

34 See W H Crossland, 'The Royal Holloway College' in *RIBA Transactions* 1887, p 142.

35 See *Builder* 17 July 1875, p 645.

36 There are constant references to James Crossland in Holloway's diary for 1877.

37 Letter 20 October 1874 in Royal Holloway Archive.

38 Letter 25 November 1874 in Royal Holloway Archive.

39 The *Graphic* reported that Holloway and his brother-in-law visited asylums in the US and Europe. See L J Whitaker, *W H Crossland: His Architectural Development*, Manchester University MA dissertation 1984, p 191.

40 Letter Holloway to Crossland 4 November 1874 in Royal Holloway Archive.

41 Letter 30 October 1874 in Royal Holloway Archive.

42 Letter 25 November 1874 in Royal Holloway Archive.

43 Letter Holloway to Crossland 4 November 1874 in Royal Holloway Archive.

44 L J Whitaker, *W H Crossland: His Architectural Development*, Manchester University MA dissertation 1984, p 200.

45 W H Crossland, 'The Royal Holloway College' in *RIBA Transactions* 1887, p 142.

46 See *Builder* 7 January 1882, p 24, though on 10 June 1882 (p 719) the same periodical said that there was accommodation for two hundred and fifty.

47 *Builder* 7 January 1882, p 24. The Prince and Princess of Wales were to become Edward VII and Queen Alexandra.

48 See memo book at the Surrey History Centre.

49 *Builder* 7 January 1882, p 23.

50 Ibid.

51 *Builder* 10 June 1882, p 719.

52 They were produced by James Imrie – see the *Builder* 7 January 1882, p 23.

53 *Tipperary Free Press* 19 February 1877.

54 *Graphic* 22 October 1881, p 414.

55 See Holloway diary 1887 for reference to gilding of roof panels.

56 See L J Whitaker, *W H Crossland: His Architectural Development*, Manchester University MA dissertation 1984, p 212.

57 *Builder* 7 January 1882, p 23.

58 See Lindsey Smith, *Thomas Holloway and The Erection of Holloway Sanatorium*, paper read to Committee of Management in 1932 and L J Whitaker, *W H Crossland: His Architectural Development*, Manchester University MA dissertation 1984, p 212. These were painted by George Morten (Nelson), Remington (Raleigh and the Duke of Marlborough) and Girodet (the remainder).

59 *Globe* 13 July 1881.

60 *Times* 16 June 1885 – See L J Whitaker, *W H Crossland: His Architectural Development*, MA Dissertation Manchester University 1984, p 211.

61 *Builder* 7 January 1882, p 23.

62 *Globe* 13 July 1881.

63 *Graphic* 22 October 1881, p 414.

64 Letter 27 October 1874 in Royal Holloway Archive.

65 This was destroyed by a fire in 1978. See L J Whitaker, *W H Crossland: His Architectural Development*, Manchester University MA dissertation 1984, p 209.

66 Designed by Fulljames & Waller. With the exception of the chapel it has since been demolished. The building was reviewed in the *Builder* of 1854 pp 509–11.

67 J Taylor, *Hospital & Asylum Architecture in England 1840–1914*, London 1991, p 157.

68 Ibid.

69 The initial trustees were Mary Ann Driver (wife's sister), Henry Driver (wife's brother), George Martin (wife's brother-in-law) and Walpole Greenwell (stockbroker) plus twenty-two others. See Lindsey Smith, *Thomas Holloway and The Erection of Holloway Sanatorium*, paper read to Committee of Management in 1932 for details.

70 When the trustees were Mary Ann Driver and George Martin. See papers at the Surrey History Centre.

71 *Country Life* 16 August 1990, p 96.

The College

No sooner had the Sanatorium started to emerge from the Surrey heathland than Holloway turned his attention to a second project, a second way of spending his vast fortune, and a second way of benefiting those of the middle classes who were less fortunate than himself.

Unlike the Sanatorium where the inspiration had been domestic, the motive force behind the second project came from the United States, and from another self-made entrepreneur, one like Holloway, who made a fortune and then set about spending it.

Matthew Vassar was born in Norfolk, emigrated in infancy to the United States,[1] and to Poughkeepsie in New York State in particular, where with time he amassed a fortune. The basis of Vassar's wealth was beer, and the Vassar & Co Brewery. He later broadened his interests, becoming a founder member of the Poughkeepsie Savings Bank, President of the Farmers and Manufacturers National Bank, and a director of the Poughkeepsie Whaling Company.

As a successful self-made businessman, Vassar amassed a small fortune, and like Holloway had no direct heir. He pleaded 'I wish somebody would tell me what to do with my money. It's the plague of my life – keeps me awake o'nights – stocks going down, banks breaking, insurance companies failing.'[2] According to Edward Linner, a recent historian of Vassar College, Matthew Vassar's initial idea was to build a hospital for the insane, an idea which then developed into the building of a large community hospital, a complex which was to be based on Guy's Hospital in Southwark. Vassar had visited Guy's during a trip to London in the 1840s, and was particularly impressed by the memorial tablet which had been erected commemorating the beneficence of Sir Thomas Guy, a man with whom Vassar claimed a distant relationship.[3] The inscription which impressed Vassar ran:

> It is peculiar to this beneficent Man to have persevered during a long course of prosperous industry in pouring forth to the wants of Others all that he had earned by labour or withheld from self-indulgence.[4]

According to Vassar's diary, what he had seen at Guy's Hospital caused him to set about searching for a project upon which he could lavish part of the fortune he had amassed, as:

> I desire to build a monument for myself, to perpetuate my own name, to do something for Po'keepsie where I have made all my money, and to do good to my fellow men.[5]

The idea of a hospital came to nothing, being supplanted by another, the idea of 'doing something for the higher education of women', an idea about which Vassar spoke in 1864, recalling how an

> interest in the subject of female education was awakened not less than twenty years ago by an intimate female friend and relative, now deceased, who conducted a seminary of long standing and character in the City... It was this fact, more than any other, and more than all others, that awakened me early to the possibility and necessity of an institution like the one we now propose.[6]

The result was a college for the education of women, an institution which would be to young women 'what Yale and Harvard are to young men', an institution which according to the first President of the college – Milo P Jewett – would have as its primary purpose the education of women so as to 'enable them to direct the mental development of the young, either at home or

Opposite: Royal Holloway College, Octagon from the South Quadrangle.

Below: Vassar College. (Collection of Dr C M Barron.)

in school'. Jewett recounted how in the 1850s there were 'two million children in the United States [who] were without the benefit of an education in their homes', and if left untaught would 'grow up to fill our Jails & penitentiaries, & to burden the honest & industrious with the expense of their pauperism & crime'.[7] Hence for Vassar the aim was to educate future mothers, those who although they would not be

> lawyers, divines & legislators... are to be the wives & mothers of lawyers & ministers, legislators & statesmen: or if never wives & mothers, thousands of them must be the Teachers of our future public men, as well as, of the masses of the people.[8]

The structural reality of this dream envisaged 'one huge college building, [one] large enough to house four hundred students... [with] a library of 10,000 volumes and a chapel for daily and Sunday worship'.[9] Plans were initially prepared by Thomas A Tefft, plans for a building which would cost $385,000, though when Tefft died in 1859 the commission passed to James Renwick who recast the design in the Second Empire French style, a design much influenced by the new Louvre building in Paris. The College opened in September 1865.

The activities at Poughkeepsie under the patronage of Matthew Vassar were a prefiguration of what was to happen at Egham under the beneficence of Thomas Holloway. Just as Vassar had considered a hospital for incurables, so also did Holloway,[10] and in both countries this idea was replaced by the concept of a college for the education of women, while the Second Empire French style which had been used at Poughkeepsie was used again in the initial designs for the College at Egham.

However, while the initial linkages were clearly with Vassar, the concept of a college for the education of women at Egham progressively assumed a momentum, style and life of its own, an independence best symbolised by the switch in precedent, a switch away from the Second Empire French style used at Poughkeepsie, to a style derived from the Loire and from the time of François I; in short from an eclectic French mixture of the nineteenth century to a French cocktail of the sixteenth century; from things current to things past, from modernism to historicism.

In mid-Victorian Britain the concept of a college for the education of women was an advanced idea, though matters were changing, a process well illustrated by Walter Shaw-Sparrow in 1891:

> The education of an English lady, when our grandparents were children, was simplicity itself. A neat and very fine handwriting was considered as necessary to her as a prim yet stately bearing: the elementary subjects, which included the dry rules of grammar and the nomenclature of book-geography, were repeated aloud till she knew them by heart: the talent of writing graceful letters was brought before her notice as one to be acquired by patience and a daily sacrifice of paper: and then she was set free from the schoolroom to encourage all manner of homely thoughts in the parlour, while mending or knitting the family socks and stockings.

> But things have changed now. The fine old school handwriting is replaced by a dashing but characteristic scrawl: letters are written at railway speed, and record the news of the hour in as few words as possible: while the elementary subjects have become the foundation for quite a library of learning. In short, the most important revolution which has taken place during the last half-century in the social life of England is surely that intellectual revolution which women have worked for themselves, and which has done much to unsettle the long-standing belief about the inferiority of the feminine intellect when compared with that of man. The late successes of lady students in competitive examinations, indeed, very convincingly prove that there is no study too difficult for our sisters to follow, not only with advantage to themselves, but, in many cases, with humiliation to us.[11]

Top: Royal Holloway College,
North Quadrangle and Centre Tower 1888.

Centre: Royal Holloway College,
North front 1886.

Bottom: Royal Holloway College,
South-east corner 1887.

Things did indeed change during the nineteenth century, but it is easy by concentrating on the changes to ignore the strong element of continuity which remained. For most of the century women occupied a subordinate and inferior position. A married woman was largely a chattel of her husband, a chattel whose responsibilities centred on the home and the moral upbringing of any children, while for the unmarried the emphasis was on a limited range of occupations, ones reserved for women and typified by the spinster teacher. While Mary Wollstonecraft made the first clear statement on the need for change as early as 1792, there was little change in the political and civil position of women until the mid-1800s when there was some limited movement to ease the disadvantages women suffered, but even then the changes were discriminatory in nature.

Chambord.

For instance, the 1839 Custody of Infants Act only gave women of unblemished character access to their children in the event of separation or divorce, and while the Matrimonial Causes Act of 1857 extended these rights through also allowing women access to divorce, this was only available in the event of a specific cause other than their husband's adultery – an inequality which was not amended until 1923. It was 1882 before married women were given the right to own property, and 1886 before they gained the right to be considered for sole guardianship of their children in the event of their husband's death. However, despite these advances women remained electorally disadvantaged until 1918 when those over 30 received the vote and it was 1928 before this right was extended to women who were 21 and over.

Educational provision for women was little different, as elementary education for girls was not provided by statute until 1870, though wealthier women fared somewhat better. The University of London admitted women from 1848; Bedford College, London, was founded in 1849; the North London Collegiate Day School in 1850 and Cheltenham Ladies' College in 1854. University provision at Oxford and Cambridge began in 1871 with the foundation of Newnham College, while in the following year Girton College was relocated from Hitchin to Cambridge.

Despite these disadvantages – or perhaps because of them – Holloway was attracted to the idea of a college for women even before work on the Sanatorium had progressed beyond the foundations. Holloway was also attracted to French Renaissance architecture, an interest he shared with Crossland, and one they jointly developed during a visit to the Loire. This interest in things French was partly inspired by T H Wyatt, one of the assessors for the initial Sanatorium designs, who – according to Crossland – had recommended Holloway to adopt 'the French Renaissance' style for his intended college, and particularly its application at Chambord.

These ideas were reinforced by Crossland who suggested 'a return to either the purer classical styles, or to the Renaissance of the 16th century', and he produced 'selected views [of the] châteaux in the valley of the Loire, as well as that of Fontainebleau'; designs which he 'submitted [to Holloway], placing Chambord first'. According to Crossland 'The effect [of these ideas] on Mr Holloway was somewhat startling', Holloway announcing that he had been advised to put the design for a college out to competition, but asking Crossland how he would approach the task if he was one of the competitors. Crossland's response was that he would

visit the Touraine, and, with an assistant, sketch and measure Chambord in the completest way... [plus] such portions of other châteaux as appeared to me useful in the study of the style and containing characteristics not found at Chambord.[12]

Again Holloway's response was unexpected. Turning to Crossland he announced 'My boy, you shall have the work; but mind, on the condition that you sketch and measure Chambord from bottom to top.'[13]

Now the decision to look to France, and specifically to the Loire, for inspiration was not uncommon during the 1870s, when interest in the Gothic Revival was starting to wane. The later Georgian and early Victorian periods were eras of rapid industrialization, periods when overall wealth increased at a geometric rate, when the focus of population shifted from the country to the town, and when the focus of wealth and influence started to shift from the aristocracy to a newly created entrepreneurial class, a class which Holloway represented. Those in this entrepreneurial stratum were anxious to assert their presence, anxious to create an architectural style that asserted that presence, but one which would also proclaim the supremacy of the era in which they lived: in short a style which did not just look to a replication of the past, but one which sought to fuse elements of the past into a style that would be unique to that age.

What evolved was a mongrel, a style based on the order and elegance of classicism, but one fused with Gothic spirit. One manifestation of this eclecticism was the Queen Anne style,[14] another was the French Château style, a mixture of sixteenth and seventeenth century French transported and modified to fit within industrial nineteenth century Britain. For the Rothschild family the style found expression at Waddesdon, so that a successful Jew could display his constitutional equality and economic dominance; while at Egham the style enabled Holloway to emulate and hopefully outdo the beneficence of Matthew Vassar, and thus achieve both respectability and immortality.

In 1873 Crossland and an assistant set out for France, 'Mr Holloway having stated his intention to join us at Chambord on hearing from us that our work was completed'. Holloway's diary records how he left Charing Cross for Paris in September, continuing on to Blois where 'Whilst standing at the door of the Hotel awaiting Breakfast I was unexpectedly accosted by Mr Wm Crossland.' Together they visited the château at Blois, and there made the decision 'that our building should be similar to the fifteenth-century work, viz, red brick with stone dressings',[15] before travelling on to Chambord where they commenced the process of measuring and drawing, a process aptly recorded by Holloway:

> Our work commenced about 9 going to the Château & remaining there until about 12-30, then to the Hotel to Breakfast and as it was very hard work going up and down so many flights of stairs we did not go to the château again until 2 remaining there until about 6-30. It was tiring work & we were always on the leg up and down.
>
> Mr Crossland had previously been before my arrival 10 days at Chambord on my account taking plans & drawings of the château so that my work consisted in referring to what they had done & to determine how much of the Château I wanted for my purpose as I intended at that time to take it as a model for building an Institution for incurables - but which idea I afterwards abandoned.[16]

For Crossland the result of these detailed examinations was a conviction that the 'Château of Chambord stands alone, in my opinion, in the elegance of its design and the beauty of its sculpture', though this conviction seems to have been shaken by visits that the trio then made to 'Cheverny, Blois again, Amboise, Chaumont, Chenonceaux, Valencay, Versailles, [and] Fontainebleau' before returning home.[17] For Holloway the trip crystallised into a determination to bring his plans to reality, a decision which he gave physical expression through his purchase of a 94-acre site from Lady Holland for £25,000 in the following year.[18]

Holloway's diary shows that his initial ideas were for a design based on Chambord, though with some modifications, as:

> The Château has two points but I only required one & I only took about half of the main roof of the Building as in its entirety it would have been far too large & too expensive for my

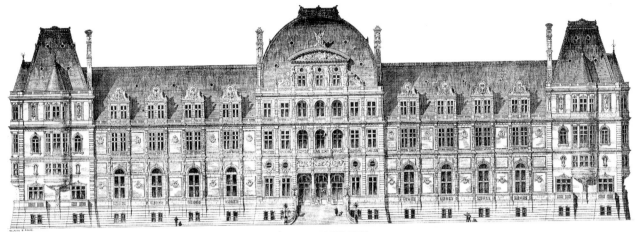

FRONT · ELEVATION ·

Crossland Original design, Building News, *21 December 1877, p 614.*

purpose. I reduced the size of the part I wanted to 2 thirds of its height & breadth & most of the parts in the same proportions. The rooms in the Château are about 20 feet 6 in & by the reduction in size that I have made they will be about 13 feet six inches.[19]

However, these ideas were initially abandoned. Crossland's prototype design – published in 1875 – had a roofline which was a rearrangement of that which had been used at Cheverny in the seventeenth century, and then for a remodelling of the Louvre by Visconti and Lefuel in 1850–7. The arrangement of the façade, its suggested division into bays, each topped by a dormer gable was probably derived from Blois, while the corbelled turrets were copied from Azay-le-Rideau, just the tall chimneys coming from Chambord.

Then, according to Crossland, in the mid-1870s Holloway 'came under the influence of certain highly educated ladies, who had been interesting themselves in the scheme',[20] namely Millicent Fawcett, Maria Grey, Dr Elizabeth Garrett Anderson, and Emily Davies. In February 1875 Holloway invited a number of them to a meeting at his Oxford Street offices; along with Sir James Kay Shuttleworth, Joshua Fitch, plus two MPs – Samuel Morley and David Chadwick – and one of the Governors of Vassar College, the Reverend William Hague; a meeting at which he presented his prototype design 'merely for the purpose of giving some idea of the style' which he had in mind.[21]

In addition to presenting his architectural preferences, Holloway explained why he had called the meeting, and why he wanted to build a women's college:

I know nothing, or next to nothing... as to the requirements or the working of a College for ladies, and... it is for this reason that I invite your kind co-operation in furnishing suggestions which, if I am wise enough to follow, I trust I shall leave behind me a monument not only of

FRONT · ELEVATION ·

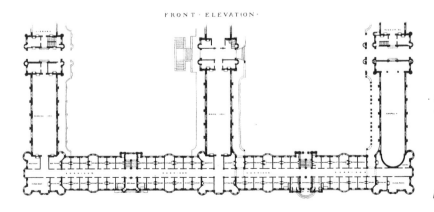

OLLOWAY ·
EGHAM ·

· COLLEGE ·
· SURREY ·
W · H · CROSSLAND ·
ARCHITECT·

Half plan of Principal Floor.

my work alone, but of your work also... I would wish that academic honours should be open to ladies in this College, and that they should have within their reach... either an MA, a DA, or even... a 'Double First'.[22]

Sir James Kay Shuttleworth suggested the College be divided into four divisions, with one segment being a teacher training college. Holloway, however, rejected these proposals, declaring that his building would be 'a University for women', and 'that or nothing'.[23] Furthermore it was to be 'a University which signifies every branch of human knowledge – where Anatomy, Botany, Mineralogy, Painting, Sculpture, Law, Divinity and I know not what else' would be taught.[24]

According to Crossland the advisers were not impressed with Holloway's architectural preferences, the female educationalists persuading him that 'the proper style of architecture to adopt was not the Renaissance, but the style in which most of the colleges at Oxford and Cambridge had been built'.[25] The result was that Crossland, Holloway and three assistants spent four weeks at Cambridge evolving an alternative design, a 'design embodying as nearly as possible all the characteristics of the larger colleges',[26] and in particular the double quadrangle plan of Trinity College, and the fifteenth-century King Edward's tower in Trinity Great Court.[27] However, during this excursion Holloway was 'attacked by a low form of fever, and another interval of inaction occurred, during which [according to Crossland] the influence of the learned ladies... lost its effect', and at his architect's 'earnest solicitations' Holloway 'returned to the Renaissance' for his inspiration.[28]

While Crossland may have had some influence over his patron's stylistic preferences and his decision to abandon Cambridge for the Loire, a more important event was the death of Jane Holloway on 25 September 1875, a disaster from which Thomas Holloway never recovered. Suddenly Holloway changed from being the leader to little more than a casual observer, from a man engrossed in the detailed planning, to one who withdrew from the world; in so doing he passed the baton of command to his brother-in-law George Martin.[29] Perhaps more importantly Holloway's final act was to seek a fitting memorial to his wife. The result has been called the Taj Mahal of Egham.[30] In the *Builder's* less emotive words 'the College is founded by the desire of the founder's wife, now deceased, and... its object is to afford the best education suitable for women of the middle and upper middle classes'.[31] Suddenly the uncertainty was ended, the style was to be from the Renaissance, from the châteaux of the Loire and the period of François I, something the *Girl's Own Paper* decreed was 'an English translation of the French Renaissance style',[32] and which the *Graphic* said was from the time of François I but 'with certain English modifications'.[33]

Crossland spent most of the next two years working out 'the plans, elevations, and details', returning occasionally to France and Belgium for further detailed inspiration.[34] The result was a return to the style exhibited at Chambord, a style which became the canvas onto which the elements from other châteaux were to be added. The skyline at Egham is a blatant copy from that atop the central donjon at Chambord, especially the elongated chimney stacks with their decorative motifs, the balustrade and the lantern which tops the central range, while the lanterns above the two entrance gateways, and the gabled dormers are variants on the style used at Chambord. This base design is then mixed with ingredients from other châteaux. The horizontal string mouldings and the engaged circular towers with their conical roofs were derived from Azay-le-Rideau, the small circular windows were copied from Cheverny, the colonnades which enhance the inner quadrangles were adaptions from those in the Cour Ovale at Fontainebleau while the staircases were taken from the François I wing at Blois.

However, it seems possible that two other châteaux also played some part in Crossland's stylistic preferences. Parts of the château at Le Lude originate from the fifteenth century, though

View from the Gardens.

Lower Quadrangle.

Picture Gallery.

Staircase.
All from *The Graphic 26 June 1886.*
Opposite: The same views today.

it had been extensively restored on several occasions, notably in the mid-eighteenth century. There is no evidence that Crossland visited the château, though the similarities between it and his designs for Egham are striking. The chimneys at both have the same triangular decoration, the cupolas are identical, there are small circular windows in the roof of both buildings, and shelled pediments top the pilaster sided gable dormers.

The other possibility is more intriguing as there is no evidence that Crossland visited the château that was being built at Vouzeron (1874–8) to the designs of Hippolyte Destailleur, an architect who was also responsible for the château being built at Waddesdon for the Rothschild family. However, it would have been unusual if Crossland had not been curious enough to visit Vouzeron, to look, learn and perhaps copy; to note the effect of combining red brick with stone; to see the effect of horizontal string mouldings, of engaged circular towers with conical roofs, of using decorative shell motifs, and perhaps most of all to see and adopt the idea of an underground tunnel linking the château with its domestic buildings which were located some distance away – all features which were to be replicated at Egham, features which perhaps suggest that the debt to Vouzeron and Destailleur may be greater than has previously been acknowledged.

Having designed the College Crossland tried out his architectural ideas on the Kirkgate Buildings which Sir John William Ramsden commissioned for the centre of Huddersfield. The Huddersfield building was started in 1878, and the foundation stone for the College was laid in 1879. The Kirkgate Buildings were finished in 1885, and the College was opened in 1886. The gabled dormers and entrance bay at Huddersfield are replicated at Egham, as are the horizontal string courses and the robustly dressed windows. Only the towers provide a distinctiveness, with German or North European precedents at Huddersfield while the Loire reigned supreme at Egham.

The first brick of the College was laid by George Martin in 1879, an occasion he used to congratulate Crossland on 'the magnificent pile about to be erected... those plans and designs on which you have bestowed so much skilful labour and attention, and which have been so thoughtfully directed throughout by Mr Holloway'.[35] The skyline was up by 1881, a 'bold arrangement' upon which – according to the *Art Journal* – the building 'depended almost entirely for effect', a silhouette which was 'broken by countless mansards, conical roofs, dormers, many-pinnacled towers, and tall elaborate chimneys'.[36]

The *Builder* ran a detailed review of the College in 1881, declaring that the building was to be 'of enormous size', one which:

> forms a double quadrangle 500 ft from east to west, and 350 ft from north to south. The main portions, which run from east to west on each side, consist of five floors, each 10 ft 6 in high, all of which... [sic] are rooms for students, professors, and class-rooms, connected by four spacious stone staircases placed equi-distant, two in each wing.[37]

The upper quadrangle would be entered through 'a spacious driving gateway' which separated the chapel on one side from a recreation hall on the other, and the gateway was 'surmounted and surrounded by suites of rooms for chiefs of departments... the whole being crowned with a clock tower, rising to a height of 130 ft from the ground'. Similarly the lower quad would be entered through an equally grand gateway, 'the tradesmen's driving gateway', with a gymnasium and racket court below a library on one side, and music rooms below a museum on the other. Again above the gateway there would be 'suites of five rooms on each floor... for heads of departments... the whole surmounted by a bell-tower 140 ft high'. Not to be outdone, the central cross range which would accommodate the dining hall and kitchens, was to be adorned with an octagonal water tower combining functionality with beauty, the whole being topped by an elaborate crown complete with winged lions, swans, crocodiles and storks.[38]

In 1887 Crossland presented a paper to the RIBA in which he described the planning and construction of the College.[39]

> The scholastic department is contained in the two main blocks, and these are connected by rooms, cloisters, and balconies. The refectory and kitchen, arranged on the usual college plan, are divided by the central hall and vestibule. The museum and library, also the recreation hall, communicate directly with the two main blocks.[40]

The intention was that no student should reside outside the College, attendance being restricted to no more than four years, and that during this time 'Each student will have [exclusive use of] two rooms – study and bedroom', and a common room would be provided 'for every six students, where they can hold tea and toast parties, or other entertainments'. The teaching staff were to be accommodated in superior rooms located in the central and corner pavilions,[41] the lecture room was to be at the south-west corner with classrooms in the other three corners, the building accommodating two hundred and fifty students, but according to Crossland 'on so liberal a scale that 50 may be added to this number', which with academics and servants would give a total population of 400.[42] Functionality was not forgotten, with an engine house,[43] laundry, gas works, coal and wood stores, located in a hollow three hundred yards from the main building and connected to the College by a tunnel which terminated below the kitchens; an arrangement which allowed the main building and its numerous fireplaces to be serviced without destroying the picturesque effect.[44]

The *Builder* presented the bald statistics of construction, reporting that '800 men [were] employed on the building', including 320 masons, with 'more than 3,000 yards... of tram-road in and around the building, seven powerful steam derrick cranes, and eleven hand cranes... sixteen two-ton hand-travellers... [and] a ten-ton steam traveller'. The finished structure they announced would contain '858 rooms, 1,912 windows, and 760 fireplaces'.[45]

The College was opened by Queen Victoria at 5.30 pm on Wednesday 30 June 1886, and the first students were admitted in October 1887. The *Builder* declared that the finished 'building generally is such an architectural success... that we willingly forget the faults of the detail', faults 'with many of the mouldings', with:

> Much of the ornament... [which is] coarse and heavy, and the proportions of many of the windows and openings are much lower than we are accustomed to consider correct. The omission of the bed-mould of the main cornice, leaving merely a row of exaggerated details, though there is some precedent for it, is not a successful device, and the capping of the small circular angle-buttresses of the main central pavilions is absolutely ugly.[46]

However, such faults were eclipsed by the good points, and in particular by the 'magnificence of the angle pavilions, the picturesqueness of the lanterns over the main entrances, the dignified sobriety of the long horizontal lines, [and] the pleasant balance of all the parts'.[47]

Holloway established a trust and trustees to oversee the working of his College,[48] decreeing that there should be an entrance examination which would include 'English language, composition, and history; the elements of Latin, French, or German, or some other foreign language; arithmetic, integral and fractional; the elements of some one branch of mathematical or physical science'; though students who had passed 'the senior local examination at Oxford or Cambridge, or the matriculation examination of the University of London, or such other examination by some competent and public authority' should be exempt.[49]

The regulations required the teaching staff to be unmarried women or widows without children. The principal, who would have 'almost absolute power', should be under forty when

Student rooms.

Royal opening 30 June 1886.

she was appointed, and would be required to retire at sixty-five.[50] Once admitted the students would not receive an education which was 'regulated by the traditions of former ages', but instead one which was 'founded on studies and sciences which the experience of modern times has shown to be most valuable'.[51] It was hoped that half the students would sit the examination of Oxford University – though they were not eligible for a degree until 1920 when the Oxford colleges recognized women – the remainder taking the examinations of the University of London, an organization which did confer degrees on women. The University of London also provided five of the governors,[52] and it was this link which was to find a more permanent arrangement in 1900 when the College was integrated as part of the University of London.[53]

Holloway's ideas on education were clear-cut, and so were his religious views, views which epitomised the age and marked a decline from the certainty of belief which existed in the early Victorian era. By the latter part of the century – for many – certainty had been replaced by doubt or clear disbelief, while for the believers there was a wider palette to chose from, a panoply of sects which ranged from high to low and from the orthodox to the non-connexional. For Holloway this plurality of belief meant that 'No professor will be required to submit to any test concerning his or her religious opinions', as 'having witnessed the hand of God in all things'. Holloway was anxious to ensure that the 'religious teaching of the college should be such as to impress most forcibly on the mind of each student her individual responsibility, and her duty to God', students being free to 'attend the service of the Church of England, or of any sect or denomination which their parents or guardians may desire'. There would be a 'simple daily service' with 'the reading of a portion of Scripture', and a suitable Sunday service, though 'no permanent chaplain shall be appointed, and no arrangement shall be made which would identify the college in any way with any particular sect or denomination of Christians'.[54]

Despite these religious restrictions Holloway provided a chapel which the *Girl's Own Paper* described as 'a most sumptuous building',[55] and one which the *Builder* and Crossland both described as being not unlike the Sistine Chapel at the Vatican.[56] The building was of six bays with an apsidal eastern end, the sculptural decoration initially being undertaken by Ceccardo Fucigna, and after his death by his assistant Boldini. The windows on either side were separated by niches in which marble statues were to be placed, statues of St Alban and the four patron saints of Britain – Saints George, Andrew, Patrick and David – plus five female saints noted for learning – Saints Scholastica, Agnes, Catherine, Ursula and Etheldreda.[57] Above the windows the ceiling contained subjects in bold relief – a style Crossland said was modelled on Fontainebleau – with Samuel and the four greater prophets on the south, and St John the Baptist and the four evangelists on the north.[58] The initial design for the apse comprised a depiction of Christ in Majesty, though this was replaced by a depiction of the creation of Eve, with three large figures below – namely Our Lord as the Good Shepherd, St Mary and St Cecilia – while the side parts of the apse were labelled with the attributes Holloway expected his students to possess, Faith, Hope and Charity on the north-east corner and Modesty, Purity and Fortitude on the south-east. The same bold relief was used along the crown of the vault where six medallions depicted the archangels – Michael, Gabriel, Raphael, Uriel, Zadkiel and Chamael – while at the western end the medallions flanking the organ contained depictions of angels playing musical instruments.[59]

A riot of coloured decoration, now sadly dimmed, was applied to the walls by Clayton & Bell with the most pronounced colours on the lower sections of the walls, an arrangement which created a form of dado between the floor and window sills, while above this the walls were painted green with red in the niches.[60]

Fucigna and Boldini produced carved keystones for the exterior of the chapel and recreation hall windows, and for the arches of the main entrance gateway. Crossland described the arrangement starting with the entrance gateway where:

on the outside [there was] Minerva, on the inside Hope. On each side are the three prophets – Moses, Ezekiel, and Elijah, opposite the three kings – Joshua, Saul, and Solomon. On the gateway towards the quadrangle are Faith on the inside and Homer on the outside. The keystones to the chapel windows are on the outside Christ, St John, St Peter, and St Paul. On the inside or quadrangle side are Pope Julius II, Mohammed (the College is undenominational), Confucius, and Savonarola. Flanking these are allegorical heads of the Elements – Fire, Earth, Air, and Water.[61]

The same symbolism was used elsewhere. The dome of the dining hall entrance contained amorini and emblems of the arts and sciences, while the pediments above the four main staircases on the insides of the quadrangles contained bas reliefs which acted as a constant reminder of Holloway and his intentions. Above the western door in the upper quad there was a depiction of poetry and science, while above the eastern door the symbolism was of commerce and medicine. In the lower quad the eastern pediment recognized the county of Surrey and its dominant agricultural activity along with a bust of Holloway which was based upon one of Napoleon in the Louvre, while that on the western pediment again reminded students who had provided the College, being a depiction of charity and education separated by the inscription 'Nil Desperandum' and the Holloway family crest. Later a large statue of Thomas and Jane was added to the lower quadrangle, with one of Queen Victoria in the upper quadrangle; both were unveiled in December 1887.[62]

The College building has been reviewed several times by notable architectural historians, once by John Betjeman and twice by Joe Mordaunt Crook, the latter concluding that 'As a symbol... as an image, as a manifestation touristique, Royal Holloway College was unbeatable. It shared all the magnificence – and inconvenience – of its principal prototype, the palatial Chambord.' The double quadrangle plan may be traditional, the sloping site confusing and inconvenient, the main entrances ineffectual – both leading into nothing more than open quadrangles – but, he concluded, 'The result is sensational.'[63]

Holloway obviously felt much the same, Crossland telling us that he 'patted me on the back and said, "well done, Mr Crossland, I am more than pleased."'[64] And so he should have been: the Holloway College survives as an icon, an icon of the founder's success, of his concern for others, of his progressiveness, and perhaps of his ego; but it also acts as an icon of Victorianism, of an age which possessed a confidence we know not how to equal, and a belief that tomorrow would undoubtedly be better than today.

Teaching and administrative staff 1887.

Queen Victoria in the chapel.
The Graphic *1886.*

Keystones.

Notes

1 He was born on 29 April 1792 and emigrated in October 1796.

2 E Linner, *Vassar:The Remarkable Growth of a Man and His College 1855-1865*, Poughkeepsie 1984, pp 17-8.

3 Ibid, p 16.

4 Ibid, p ix.

5 Ibid, p 17.

6 Ibid, p 15.

7 Ibid, p 21.

8 Ibid.

9 Ibid, p 26.

10 See Holloway diary for 16 September 1873 at Surrey History Centre.

11 Walter Shaw-Sparrow, 'The Royal Holloway College Picture Gallery' in *Magazine of Art* 1891.

12 W Crossland, 'The Royal Holloway College' in *RIBA Transactions* 1887, pp 142–3.

13 Ibid.

14 A mixture of English, Belgian, Dutch, French early Renaissance with English vernacular.

15 W Crossland, 'The Royal Holloway College' in *RIBA Transactions* 1887, p 143.

16 Holloway Diary for 1873 at Surrey History Centre.

17 W Crossland, 'The Royal Holloway College' in *RIBA Transactions* 1887, p 143.

18 J M Crook, 'Holloway's Architect and Château' in M Moore (ed), *Centenary Lectures*, Egham 1988, p 33. The site was purchased in May 1874.

19 Holloway Diary for 1873 at Surrey History Centre.

20 W Crossland, 'The Royal Holloway College' in *RIBA Transactions* 1887, p 143.

21 J M Crook 'Holloway's Architect and Château' in M Moore (ed), *Centenary Lectures*, Egham 1988, p 33.

22 Caroline Bingham, 'Founder and Founding' in M Moore (ed), *Centenary Lectures*, Egham 1988, p 17.

23 Letter Holloway to Crossland 3 March 1875 in Royal Holloway Archive.

24 Letter Holloway to Crossland 20 February 1875 in Royal Holloway Archive.

25 W Crossland, 'The Royal Holloway College' in *RIBA Transactions* 1887, pp 143–4.

26 Ibid, p 144.

27 J M Crook, 'Holloway's Architect and Château' in M Moore (ed), *Centenary Lectures*, Egham 1988, p 35.

28 W Crossland, 'The Royal Holloway College' in *RIBA Transactions* 1887, p 144.

29 George Martin changed his name to Martin-Holloway and was knighted at Osborne House by Queen Victoria in 1887 as a reward for his contribution.

30 J M Crook, 'Holloway's Architect and Château' in M Moore (ed), *Centenary Lectures*, Egham 1988, p 35.

31 *Builder* 8 October 1881, p 450. The *Illustrated London News* also credited Jane Holloway with the idea - see issue of 3 July 1886.

32 *Girl's Own Paper* 17 July 1886.

33 *Graphic* 10 July 1886.

34 W Crossland, 'The Royal Holloway College' in *RIBA Transactions* 1887, p 144.

35 *Surrey Advertiser* 15 September 1879.

36 *Art Journal* January 1885.

37 *Builder* 8 October 1881, p 449.

38 The *Art Journal* reported that the crown paralleled St Giles Cathedral in Edinburgh, and the spire of St Nicholas in Newcastle, but with proportions that reminded them of Wren's bell tower at Christ Church in Oxford – see *Art Journal* January 1885.

39 The General Conference of Architects visited the site on 3 May 1887.

40 W Crossland, 'The Royal Holloway College' in *RIBA Transactions* 1887, p 145.

41 See *Builder* 8 October 1881, pp 449–50.

42 W Crossland, 'The Royal Holloway College' in *RIBA Transactions* 1887, p 145.

43 For the generation of electricity.

44 See *Art Journal* January 1885 for details.

45 *Builder* 10 June 1882, p 719.

46 *Builder* 3 July 1886, p 36.

47 Ibid.

48 There were to be three trustees for the property, initially George Martin-Holloway, H Driver-Holloway and David Chadwick, plus nine governors who included HRH Prince Frederick Christian and the Archbishop of Canterbury, five of the governors being appointed by the University of London.

49 *Builder* 8 October 1881, p 450.

50 *Builder* 8 October 1881, p 450 and *Girl's Own Paper* 17 July 1886.

51 Ibid.

52 See *Illustrated London News* 3 July 1886.

53 Men were admitted after 1945, starting with postgraduates, and then undergraduates, such that today the college admits both male and female students.

54 *Builder* 8 October 1881, p 450.

55 *Girl's Own Paper* 17 July 1886.

56 *Builder* 2 April 1887, p 497 & W Crossland, 'The Royal Holloway College' in *RIBA Transactions* 1887, pp 147–8.

57 The statues do not exist but the niches are still labelled with the names of the saints. On the north there are niches for Saints David, Agnes, Patrick, Etheldreda and George, while on the south are located those for Saints Ursula, Andrew, Scholastica, Alban and Catherine. Richard Williams tells me that the statues may never have been installed.

58 On the north the reliefs are of Mark, Luke, John the Baptist, Matthew and then John while on the south are depicted Elijah, Saul, Jeremiah, David and Moses.

59 See W Crossland, 'The Royal Holloway College' in *RIBA Transactions* 1887, pp 147–8.

60 Ibid.

61 Ibid. Crossland is slightly inaccurate as the keystones on the north side of the chapel are of St John, Christ, St Peter and St George – and not St Paul. There are two allegorical heads on each side of the chapel, one at each end of the main depictions. For the recreation hall the depictions were of Dante, Aeschylus, Molière and Shakespeare on the quadrangle side and Handel, Rossini, Schiller and Machiavelli on the outside.

62 The statue was carved by Count Gleichen, the Prince Victor of Hohenlohe – whose mother was Queen Victoria's half-sister – as was that of Queen Victoria in the upper quadrangle – see *Daily News* 17 December 1887. The statue of Queen Victoria was unveiled by Princess Christian and that of the Holloways by Lord Thring who was a governor.

63 J M Crook, 'Mr Holloway's Château' in *Country Life* 9 October 1986, p 1124.

64 W Crossland, 'The Royal Holloway College' in *RIBA Transactions* 1887, p 148.

The Picture Gallery

Thomas Holloway was responsible for two picture collections, one housed at Tittenhurst, the other at the College. The former was largely dominated by Old Masters, and comprised paintings which had been part of the collection held by the King of the Netherlands and exhibited at Manchester in 1857,[1] plus seventy-eight paintings Holloway acquired in 1869 when he bought Broomfield Hall from Captain Joseph Dingwall. After Holloway's death these latter paintings passed to his sister-in-law, with two subsequently ending up as part of the Frick Collection in New York, while the majority were sold at auction in 1912.

However, it was the collection of modern paintings which Holloway acquired for his College that largely survives, just three items having been sold in recent years to fund maintenance of the building.[2] Again the inspiration for such a collection came from the United States and from Vassar College in particular.

Vassar had a picture gallery and – for Holloway – so also must its English echo. The similarities are striking as an 1865 description of Vassar illustrates:

> Opposite the gallery of the Chapel is the entrance to the Art Gallery. This admits us to a room thirty feet in width and ninety-six feet in length, lighted from a dome in the centre that rises about forty feet above the floor, a sky-light in each wing, and windows along the western front of the College. In the greater proportion of the apartment, the walls, from the floor well up towards the cornice, are hung with pictures, all adapted by their size and character to the purposes of instruction.[3]

The Vassar collection was purchased from the Reverend Magoons by Matthew Vassar in 1864 for $20,000. Magoons was one of the initial trustees of Vassar College, one who had amassed a private collection of paintings, drawings and artifacts, plus an extensive art history library, largely gathered together during visits to Europe, and particularly to England, in 1844–5 and 1854.[4]

Crossland's initial designs for the College at Egham show a recreation hall in the space now occupied by the picture gallery, an arrangement which was changed to match what existed at Vassar, and to house a collection which Holloway intended should be representative of modern British painting. While the College was being built the paintings were hung at the Sanatorium; and the switch from recreation hall to picture gallery was not achieved without some problems. The absence of top light and the existence of large south facing windows makes viewing of those paintings on the north side difficult at certain times of the day, though the hanging space was improved in 1903 when the pilasters were removed from the lower part of the walls.

While the College has on a number of occasions lent paintings to exhibitions in Britain and overseas, the whole collection has only been removed from the gallery on one occasion, namely during November and December 1981 when they were exhibited in London in aid of the Victorian Society while the picture gallery was redecorated.[5]

What makes the collection unique is that the paintings were all purchased over a two-year period, and so represent a microcosm of the High Victorian art market, being examples of those works which Holloway and his contemporaries considered worthy of collection. In most galleries the paintings on display represent the works that the curatorial staff believe will be attractive to a modern audience, whereas what you see in the Holloway collection are those paintings which were popular in the early 1880s. For us some will still be attractive, others less so, and to our late twentieth-century eyes some will simply seem indifferent.

The Picture Gallery,
set up for a function 2005.

In October 1881 the *Builder* magazine announced that 'Mr Holloway contemplates the formation of a picture gallery in the college and the paintings he has already purchased for the purpose show that it will be a collection of no common kind.'[6] Between 28 May 1881 and 2 June 1883 Holloway acquired some seventy-seven paintings, all but five bought at auction,[7] the cheapest costing just £23/2/0d, the dearest being the *Babylonian Marriage Market* by Edwin Longsden Long and *Man Proposes, God Disposes* by Edwin Landseer, both of which cost £6,615 and created saleroom records.

The Holloway paintings are largely a springtime collection, sixty-four were acquired in April or May, forty-four in 1883. The collection process started in May 1881 when five paintings were purchased – including the Landseer – for £18,847/10/0d, one more following in June, seven in July, one in August and another one in September. The same momentum was maintained in 1882 with two paintings arriving in March, six in April and nine in May, though it was 1883 before matters reached a fever pitch of activity when twenty-four paintings were bought in April, twenty in May, with the final addition in June.

Holloway was accused of inflating prices, despite using a non-de-plume and his less well known brother-in-law as his agent. In 1881 *The Times* leader reported 'Saturday's splendid extravagance',[8] and in May 1883 they reported that:

> The presence of late of an amateur buyer with apparently unlimited means at [his] command, has created no small excitement on the great Fine Art Exchange in King Street [Christie's], and quite a flutter among the artists, who never could have dreamed of such prices for their pictures. Such an impetus has been given to the commercial value of good pictures as has not been seen since the memorable Gillott sale ten years ago, but artists must note that it is only pictures of first-rate merit that command these high prices.[9]

However, the intervention of a serious buyer was acknowledged as beneficial, Holloway's obituary in the *Art Journal* declaring that 'The death of Mr Thomas Holloway, on the 26th of December, removes from the world of Art a collector who, had he commenced at an earlier stage in his career, would probably have amassed a gallery of modern pictures unequalled in its cost and size.' [10]

The collection is almost exclusively of secular scenes, and does not contain any true Pre-Raphaelite paintings, though two paintings in the collection were produced by Millais who was one of the founding Pre-Raphaelites. The paintings were all modern works, and of sufficient merit to warrant a viewing by Queen Victoria, who wrote in her diary on 30 June 1886:

> We were taken to the Picture Gallery, where there are fine specimens of modern art and many well known pictures, such as *The 2 Princes in the Tower* by Millais, Landseer's *Palace Bears*, Frith's *Derby Day*, Long's *Marriage Market*, etc.[11]

Ironically two paintings which today form part of the collection do not hang in the picture gallery, but in the hallway outside, namely those produced in 1845 by William Scott of Thomas and Jane Holloway. Holloway was forty-five years old at the time and his wife thirty-one, but while Jane is depicted in an unflattering style, her husband appears more youthful than his age would suggest; a change in image that no doubt owed much to the fact that it was Thomas Holloway who was paying.

Perhaps the most famous painting in the collection, and jointly one of the most expensive, is *Man Proposes, God Disposes*, a depiction which was painted by Sir Edwin Landseer in 1864. Landseer was an enormously successful painter, much approved of by Queen Victoria who owned a large collection of his works. When Holloway bought this painting the price he paid set saleroom records for Landseer's work, records which were not exceeded until Agnews bought

The Monarch of the Glen, an image appropriated by John Dewar & Sons Ltd who continue to use it on their whisky bottle labels.

The subject matter of *Man Proposes, God Disposes* centres around the expedition – led by Sir John Franklin in the mid-1840s – which attempted to locate the north-west passage linking the Atlantic and Pacific across the pole, and one in which Franklin and his fellow explorers perished. There followed a series of attempts to find the ships *Erebus* and *Terror* which formed the basis of the expedition, along with the crews and explorers numbering over one hundred.

This was clearly a subject that interested Holloway, as those of his personal papers which are held by the Surrey History Centre, contain details and press reports on several of the seventeen search expeditions which were mounted. Eventually Lieutenant W R Hobson from the naval vessel *Fox* discovered the remnants of the expedition on King William Island, together with records showing that *Erebus* and *Terror* had become ice bound on 12 September 1846, were then deserted on 22 April 1847, Franklin dying on 11 June along with six other officers and fifteen men.[12]

The Landseer painting was produced in 1864 for Edward John Coleman of Stoke Park, Buckinghamshire, receiving many complimentary reviews, but also criticism; its subject matter being considered somewhat indelicate, as the widowed Lady Jane Franklin was still alive. The canvas has somewhat unusual dimensions, being wide in relation to its height, and depicts two polar bears ravaging the remains of the expedition. The scene is dissected diagonally by a broken mast, and the linkage to Franklin is made through the depiction of a Red Ensign and a telescope; the latter referring to a discovery made during one of the search expeditions. Neither bear is painted in full, the depiction relying heavily upon suggestion, not just a suggestion of the fate Franklin and his crew suffered, but also a scene that is suggestive of human vanity in an age of progress, and of the futility of such endeavour in the face of God's heavenly power. Hence it became common for the painting to be covered with a Union Jack during examinations so as to protect those students sitting near it from its powerful negative influences.

Equally famous was Sir John Everett Millais, one of the founding Pre-Raphaelites, and an artist who gained significant distinction and prestige in later life.[13] The Pre-Raphaelites rebelled against the artistic conventions of early nineteenth-century Britain, advocating the introduction of serious, didactic depictions that were painted in detail and majored on a return to nature. A fellow founder member of the Pre-Raphaelites – William Holman Hunt – claimed that in later life all his colleagues had deviated from these initial truths in search of wealth and influence, and certainly the two paintings Holloway purchased follow a different technique from that originally advocated by the youthful reformers. However, Millais was fifty when he produced these two works, and over the intervening thirty years since the formation of the Brotherhood, his style had adapted to the changing needs of a growing Victorian art market. Hence these particular paintings are representative examples of the mature Millais style rather than of the more idealistic principles he initially espoused.

The two paintings are *The Princes in the Tower* which was produced in 1878, and *Princess Elizabeth in Prison at St James's* which followed in 1879. The former shows the two infant sons of the late King Edward IV who were imprisoned in 1483 by their uncle, Richard Duke of Gloucester, who then usurped the throne as Richard III; the boys were Edward V aged thirteen, and his younger brother Richard Duke of York aged ten. The other painting is of the second daughter of Charles I and Queen Henrietta Maria, imprisoned at St James as a child, and later transferred to Carisbrooke Castle on the Isle of Wight where she died aged fifteen.

The princes are shown immediately before their death, with the stairs and the general blackness being used to create an atmosphere of anticipation and fear, while the princess is shown writing to the Parliamentary Commissioners asking that her faithful governess be allowed

The Princes in the Tower, *1878*
Sir John Everett Millais.

Applicants for Admission to a Casual Ward, 1874 Sir Luke Fildes.

to serve her in prison. Millais's daughter acted as the model for the princess, and the connection to Charles I was reinforced by his portrait which hangs on a rear wall.

Conventional wisdom usually decreed that the princes were suffocated, though here Millais seems to suggest that they were murdered on a staircase, a possibility which was given substance by the discovery of two skeletons below a staircase of the White Tower in 1674. There is some debate about the pictorial precedents which were used, the most likely source being a painting by Paul Delaroche entitled *Edward V and the Duke of York in the Tower* which was part of the Wallace Collection, and almost certainly known to Millais.

In his later life Millais frequently made children the centre-piece of his paintings, though usually in a sentimental setting. These two works represent children as history subjects, a genre also used by Millais for his famous *Boyhood of Raleigh*, a painting which hangs in the Tate and which was painted at Budleigh Salterton, a South Devon seaside resort visited by Millais.[14]

Two paintings in the collection illustrate a late Victorian dilemma, namely how to deal with those at the bottom of the social order, those who failed, those who starved, and those who threatened to be a drain on society; in short those who comprised an underclass, a social residuum. In the early part of the Victorian period a moral certainty decreed that such failure was the result of idleness or a lack of temperance, the correct treatment being incarceration in workhouses, establishments which aimed to reform through an uncharitable environment; as the alternative – charity – would only pauperise the recipient. As the century progressed so this certainty gave way to doubt, and then to an acceptance that failure was often the result of causes beyond the powers of any individual.

Luke Fildes' *Applicants for Admission to a Casual Ward* epitomises this changed attitude. Painted in 1874, it depicted the residuum of urban society queuing for admission to a workhouse where the fortunate ones would receive food and shelter for the night. The picture started in 1869 as an illustration for the *Graphic*, an illustration Fildes based on a scene he had seen when he first came to London in 1863. Then in 1874 Fildes produced an oil painting which was exhibited at the Royal Academy; its origins he described thus:

[I] used to ramble about a great deal on winter evenings visiting the Police Station where the applicants assembled with the hope of getting an order for the district workhouse and the people ranged themselves against the wall of the Police Yard taking up their stations in the order in which they arrived – Of course the earlier arrivals had the better chance, though the Inspectors used their discretion in selecting those for reasons they thought most deserving, and, in many cases no provision whatever was made to shelter the people from the inclement weather during the weary time of waiting.[15]

Another depiction of social realism is provided by Frank Holl's *Newgate: Committed for Trial*, a painting which was based on a scene in Newgate Prison, where a friend of the artist was the Governor, and where he had experienced the scene he depicted, one of that:

part of Newgate prison, called the cage – in which prisoners whilst on trial are permitted at certain hours, & on certain days, to see their friends – on the inner side the prisoners are placed, & in the passage – their friends are conducted to them when their relations or friends are at once brought out – A Warden walks between the 2 gratings, who can hear and see everything that takes place between the friend & prisoner – It is particularly impressive for scenes of such pathos & agony of mind on both sides.[16]

Holl said 'I shall never forget the impression... [the scene] made upon me',[17] and clearly his sympathies lie with the prisoner who is shown reaching tentatively towards his wife and children, and particularly with the young mother and child who occupy centre stage and are illuminated as the mother stares wistfully past the bars of the cage.

A complete contrast is provided by Briton Riviere's *Sympathy*, a painting representative of the sentimentalized art which so fascinated late Victorians. It was painted in 1877, Riviere's daughter being the model for the girl, who is shown confiding in her only true friend. However, the critics were divided just as modern day viewers may also be; *Punch* satirising the scene, while Ruskin was particularly complimentary about the way the dog, girl and carpet were depicted.

Perhaps the most famous painting in the collection is *The Railway Station* by William Powell Frith, a painting which depicts the various human types and social classes that constituted urban, and particularly London life. This is one of three similar works produced by Frith, all of which show a cross-section of Victorian society. The first – *Ramsgate Sands* – was painted in 1854 and is now in the Royal Collection. Here the scene is of a crowd of city dwellers who were gathered on the beach at Ramsgate, the town displayed in the background, a scene only made possible by the railway. The second is *Derby Day*, a painting produced in 1858, which now hangs in the Tate, and shows a cross-section of Victorians enjoying the celebrations which accompanied the annual Derby races, another event which relied upon the railways for its popular appeal.

The painting Holloway bought was produced in 1862, and supposedly set at Paddington station where the travellers were preparing to depart on the waiting train. However, the primary object of the painting is yet again the creation of a backcloth against which Frith can depict a range of different characters, including an Italian Count who is arguing with a cab driver, and a criminal who is being arrested. In the centre the Frith family is depicted, a triangular arrangement in which Mrs Frith is kissing one of her sons, while the two edges of the painting are occupied by a somewhat indistinct depiction of the man who commissioned the work – Louis Victor Flatow. He is shown standing beside the engine, while on the other side the criminal is flanked by two City of London policemen – Detective-sergeants Michael Haydon and James Brett.

Holloway got something of a bargain when he bought Frith's *Railway Station* for £2,000, as the painting was originally commissioned by Flatow's Gallery in the Haymarket, Flatow paying £4,000 for the painting plus another £750 for the right to exhibit it, afterwards selling it on to Henry Graves & Co for £16,300. The painting was an instant success; in 1862 it was exhibited

Sympathy, *1877 Briton Riviere.*

at various locations in Britain, then in 1872 it appeared at the London International Exhibition. In 1876 it was displayed in Philadelphia, and then in Paris during 1878 before passing to Holloway in 1883.

Above: The Railway Station, *1862* *William Powell Frith.*

Several paintings, such as *Expectation: Interior of a Cottage with a Mother and Children* by Frederick Hardy and *Taking Rest* by Thomas Faed, depict women in their role as mothers, depictions which accord with popular Victorian attitudes. However, Holloway clearly intended that his College should challenge this accepted role by giving to women an education which would enable them to compete with men in the non-domestic sphere. In the picture collection this challenge is represented by John Callcott Horsley's *The Banker's Private Room: Negotiating a Loan*. Here the pictorial space is divided with two men on the right and two women on the left.

Below: The Banker's Private Room: Negotiating a Loan, *1870* *John Callcott Horsley.*

The principal characters are seated at a desk over which one of the women is reaching, her hand breaking the invisible dividing line between the two, and so intruding into the male space and male domain. Meanwhile the other characters on each side look on, the male exhibiting signs of surprise, while the female and a loyal dog sit below what appears to be a painting of *The Temptation of St Anthony*,[18] a depiction which surely suggests that it was not just education which could enhance the female armoury in the battle for equality.

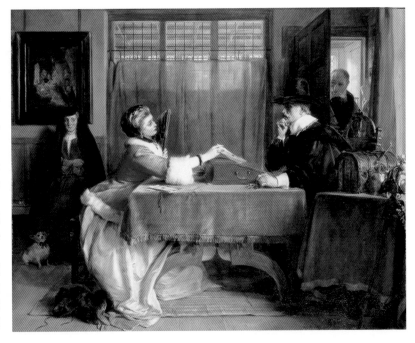

More perplexing as a subject considered suitable for a women's college is the *Babylonian Marriage Market* by Edwin Long, a painting produced in 1875, and acquired by Holloway for a record breaking £6,615 in May 1882. In a Babylonian marriage market the eligible girls are arranged in descending

order of beauty, and this is how Long arranges them in this painting, with the prettiest on the left, then in descending order of beauty until one reaches the girl who is neither 'betwixt nor between', who sits in the centre of the group, and who stares out of the painting. Then on the right hand side are arranged those girls who lack beauty, starting with the least disadvantaged and ending with a girl who hides her face in shame.

The girls were then auctioned as potential wives, the prettiest going under the hammer first and fetching the highest price. She was followed by the next prettiest who raised a somewhat smaller price, until the one who is neither 'betwixt nor between' is given away free. After this those girls who are lacking in beauty are auctioned, each giving a dowry to the husband who will accept her, the size of the dowry increasing in step with the increased lack of beauty. Such a system was considered sensible as it meant that every woman could have a husband, and every

man a wife irrespective of wealth or beauty, attributes over which one has only limited influence.

To buy such a picture for a college dedicated to the education of women seems unusual, and for it to be jointly one of the most expensive pictures in the collection seems even more unusual, facts which suggest that Victorian female sensibilities were less delicate than those of some of their twentieth-century sisters.

The Holloway collection is unique, not just because so few British universities have anything to equal it, but because it is a time capsule of Victorian taste: it displays those paintings which were popular in the early 1880s without any of the selective editing that occurs in modern art galleries. There may be insufficient wall space, the lighting may be far from ideal, the use of reflective glass annoying, but the collection rises above these problems, containing paintings of great merit within a whole that is unique.

Notes

1   At the Art Treasures Exhibition.

2   These were Turner's *Van Tromp going about to please his Masters* which was sold to the Getty Museum in California, Gainsborough's *Peasants going to Market* and Constable's *Sketch for View on the Stour, near Dedham* both of which went to a private collector.

3   E R Linner, *Vassar:The Remarkable Growth of a Man and His College 1855–1865*, Poughkeepsie 1984, p 144.

4   Ibid, pp 109, 150, 161–2 & 190.

5   A few paintings were not included in this exhibition, being on loan elsewhere.

6   *Builder* 8 October 1881, p 450.

7   Four were purchased from the Fine Art Society or Graves & Co, and one by Moreland from the Earl of Dunmore – see Jeannie Chapel, *Victorian Taste*, Egham 1982, p 12.

8   Jeannie Chapel, *Victorian Taste*, Egham 1982, p 13.

9   Ibid.

10   Ibid, p 14.

11   Ibid.

12   See *Daily Telegraph* 21 May 1895 plus various documents at the Surrey History Centre.

13   He became President of the Royal Academy and was knighted.

14   He lived in a house on the seafront that belonged to Lady Rolle.

15   Jeannie Chapel, *Victorian Taste*, Egham 1982, p 85.

16   Ibid, p 96.

17   Ibid.

18   Ibid, p 100.

The Conclusion

It is over a hundred years since the Holloway Sanatorium and College became structural realities, yet both buildings continue to serve contemporary needs. Holloway made his fortune in an age which experienced greater change and economic progress than any other before or since, though an age in which the ravages of ill health remained an ever-present reminder of man's human frailty. To this arena came Holloway with his patent medicines, medicines that promised health to a population which could afford to indulge the dream despite its intrinsic falsity.

However, having catered to a dream Holloway set about having dreams of his own, dreams that attempted to change the lot of the disadvantaged middle classes. His first dream attempted to provide a more secure remedy to the mental woes of life than did his patent medicines, while his second sought to change the social hierarchy, to elevate the long-repressed female, and to place her in a position where she could challenge the long-standing ethos of male supremacy.

While Holloway's dreams may have been a touch unusual, their execution was spectacular. The Sanatorium was no ordinary sanatorium, but one whose lavish decoration challenged, and in many cases eclipsed, those manifestations of corporate progress, the town halls. Similarly his College was no ordinary college, but one whose architectural motifs were spectacular, outdoing the Rothschilds and all the other self-made Victorian tycoons at their own game. However, for Holloway even that was not enough, and there followed a picture collection which had few if any rivals – Holloway and his age encapsulated in oil and canvas.

Throughout there was Crossland, a shadowy figure, always short of money, always committed to two women. Crossland who had made a name for himself in Yorkshire and Lancashire, but who was tempted south by Holloway and his dreams, dreams to which Crossland gave physical expression, and which stand as a lasting memorial to both these great Victorians.

Bibliography

Manuscripts and unpublished material:

Royal Holloway Archive
Royal Institute of British Architects
Surrey History Centre
Public Record Office Census Returns
L J Whitaker, *W H Crossland*, MA dissertation Manchester University, 1984

Published Primary Sources and Periodicals:

Ecclesiologist 1841–68
Builder 1843–
Building News 1855–
Rochdale Observer 21 August 1871
Old Cornwall iv 1943–50

Published Secondary Sources:

Anon, *The Story of Thomas Holloway (1800–1883)*, Glasgow: Private Publication, 1933.

C Bingham, *The History of Royal Holloway College 1886–1986*, London: Constable, 1987.

C Bingham, 'The Founder and the Founding of Royal Holloway College' in *Centenary Lectures 1886–1986*, M Moore (ed), Egham: Royal Holloway & Bedford New College, 1988.

Jeannie Chapel, *Victorian Taste*, London: Royal Holloway College, 1982.

C Cunningham, *Victorian & Edwardian Town Halls*, London: Routledge & Kegan Paul, 1981.

A Harrison-Barbet, *Thomas Holloway: Victorian Philanthropist*, Egham: Royal Holloway, University of London, 1994.

A Harrison-Barbet, *Thomas Holloway: Victorian Philanthropist*, St Austell: Lyfrow Trelyspen, 1990.

J Mordaunt Crook, 'Mr Holloway's Château', *Country Life* 9 October 1986, pp 1122–4.

J Mordaunt Crook, 'Mr Holloway's Architect and Mr Holloway's Château' in *Centenary Lectures 1886–1986*, M Moore (ed), Egham: Royal Holloway & Bedford New College, 1988.

Harriet Richardson (ed), *English Hospitals 1660–1949: A Survey of their Architecture and Design*, Swindon: Royal Commission on the Historical Monuments of England, 1998.

A Saint & R Holder, 'Holloway Sanatorium: A Conservation Nightmare' in *Victorian Society Annual 1993*, London: Victorian Society, 1994.

J Sharples, *Rochdale Town Hall*, Rochdale: Rochdale Metropolitan Borough Council, undated.

G Stamp (ed), G G Scott, *Personal and Professional Recollections*, Stamford: Paul Watkins, 1995.

J Taylor, *Hospital and Asylum Architecture in England 1840–1914*, London: Mansell Publishing, 1991.

Opposite: Statue of Queen Victoria in the North Quadrangle.

Almondbury:	All Saints (restoration)	1872–6
	Nettleton's Almshouses	1861–3
Birstall:	St Peter (rebuilding)	1863–70
Bradley:	St Thomas	1859–63
Copley:	S Stephen	1861–7
Crosshill, Nr Sutton:	S Thomas	1868–9
Dewesbury:	S ? (pulpit)	1865
Egham:	Royal Holloway College	1879–86
Flockton:	S James	1866–9
Halifax:	Akroydon	1859–
	Stable	1859
Hawnby:	All Saints (restoration)	1863
Hopton:	Parsonage	1862–3
Hoylandswaine:	St John Evangelist	1867–9
Huddersfield:	Art College	?
	Byram Arcade	1878–81
	Concert Hall	1873
	George Hotel laundry & kitchens	1873–4
	Hillhouse, School	1861–2
	Kirkgate Buildings	1878–85
	Longley Hall	1871–5
	Marshfield villas, Edgarton	1868
	Netheroyd Hill, Sunday School	1856
	New Market (unexecuted)	1869
	Post Office, Northumberland Street	1873–6
	Ramsden Estate Offices & adjacent buildings	1868–74
	S (unexecuted)	1862
	S Andrew, Leeds Road	1869–71
	S Bartholomew, Marsden (unexecuted)	1866
	St Andrew parsonage (unexecuted)	1875
	St Andrew's School	c1869
	St John the Evangelist, Newsome	1871–2
	Vicarage, Newsome	1874–5

	Woodfield House, Lockwood, Gate House	1863
Kellington:	S Edmund (restoration)	1866–70
Leeds:	Block of Houses in Belle Vue Road	1863
	Christ Church, Upper Armley (unexecuted)	1867
	Elland, S Mary (restoration)	1865–6
	Hotel at Elland	1864
	House in Cookridge St	1863
	Mechanics' Institute (competition entry)	1860
	S Chad, Far Headingley	1867–8
	Shops & Houses at Elland	1865
Lockington:	S Mary (restoration)	1865
London:	Highgate Cemetry Memorial	1882
	Criterion Tavern Piccadilly (unexecuted)	1871
Masham:	Christ Church (restoration)	1866
Manchester:	Exchange Building (competition)	1866
Methley:	Parsonage	1865
Middlesmoor:	S Chad (restoration)	1865–6
Mold Green:	Christ Church	1862–3
Ossett:	Holy Trinity	1862–7
Ripon:	SS John & Mary Chapels	?
Rishworth:	Lodge for Henry Savile	1868
Rochdale:	S Chad (restoration)	1870–2
	River Wall Parapets	1868
	Town Hall	1864–71
Sheffield:	Broomhall, St Mark	1868–71
Staincliffe:	Christ Church	1865–7
	Vicarage	1869
Sunninghill:	St Michael (Holloway chapel)	1888
Unknown:	School of Art (unexecuted)	pre 1873
Virginia Water:	Sanitorium	1871–85
Womersley:	S Martin (restoration)	

In compiling this list of commissions I am indebted to Mr Edward Law of Kilkenny in Ireland for permission to draw upon his researches, and his list of Crossland commissions. Mr Law's papers are deposited in the RIBA Library.

Over: Holloway's ointment pots.

Inside front and back cover:
Original wallpaper from the Boardrooms,
Royal Holloway, University of London.

Back cover: The North Tower,
Founder's Building, Royal Holloway,
University of London.